Ship Names: Origins and Usages during 45 Centuries

Ship Names

Origins and Usages during 45 Centuries

Don H. Kennedy

Published for The Mariners Museum

Newport News, Virginia

by the University Press of Virginia, Charlottesville

THE UNIVERSITY PRESS OF VIRGINIA
Copyright © 1974 by Don H. Kennedy

First published 1974

Museum Publication Number 31
Photographs by the author

Frontispiece: The charter fishing boat *Mona Lisa*
is well identified through the large letters
on her bow and on front of the pilothouse.

ISBN: 0-8139-0531-1
Library of Congress Catalog Card Number: 73-94274
Printed in the United States of America

To Nina

Preface

Tʜɪs book traces the ship naming tradition through primitive, ancient, and classical times and then briefly through several European cultures, all as background for an examination of ship names as used primarily in Great Britain and the United States. Although several works deal with naval ships and their names, no book has hitherto been available on ship names in general.

The term *ship* is used loosely in its generic sense, whether applied to small or large vessels, ancient or modern, except in a few instances where a specific meaning will be evident. Usually ship names are given in modern spelling and foreign names in their English equivalents. The definite article, properly a part of many foreign names, is dropped. Dates in parentheses after names are build or launch dates and are believed to be correct, although many names and dates have come from secondary sources. The term *register* is used in a general sense; the distinction between enrollment and registration is usually disregarded.

Lloyd's Register of Shipping has been used as the basic modern reference; it is the oldest such periodical compilation and attempts to list all the world's merchant shipping of 100 gross tons or more, as well as smaller vessels classed with Lloyd's. Over half the world's large commercial vessels are said to be so classed, because such a listing (as is the case also with *The Record of the American Bureau of Shipping*) is advantageous when insuring, chartering, or selling a vessel.

Persons familiar with ships will be able to think of many appropriate names not cited in the text to illustrate the wide variety in ship naming. Usually the problem was what to reject to limit names to a few apt examples from different periods. While many famous ship names were chosen, preference often went to names less well known. Names chosen were in most cases typical, although many that were unusual or unique could not be overlooked.

Special thanks for assistance are due to several persons, particularly to Giorgio Buccellati, John B. Callender, and Miriam Lichtheim, all of the University of California, Los Angeles. Dr. Buccellati translated the Akkadian ship names and Dr. Callender many of the Egyptian ship names. Any errors in conclusions regarding such names are mine. Dr. Lichtheim kindly aided in numerous ways. Generous assistance was given by Captain K. O. Meyer, chief pilot, Port of Los Angeles. John Lyman, of the University of North Carolina, and J. S. Morrison, president of University College, Cambridge, were both helpful. Valuable information came from Rear Admiral W. L. Read, United States Navy, and Captain J. H. B. Smith, Naval History Division, United States Navy. Robert H. Burgess, curator of The Mariners Museum, assumed a considerable burden involving publication details.

Contents

Ship Names: Origins and Usages during 45 Centuries

Abbreviations for Books Cited in the Text

BWN   T. D. Manning and C. F. Walker, *British Warship Names* (London, 1959).

Hakluyt   Richard Hakluyt, *Voyages*, 8 vols., Everyman's Library (1962).

Jane's   Raymond V. B. Blackman, ed., *Jane's Fighting Ships 1968–69* (New York, 1968).

Lloyd's   *Lloyd's Register of Shipping 1970–71*, 2 vols. (London, 1970).

MVUS68 *Merchant Vessels of the United States, 1968* (Washington, D.C., 1969).

CHAPTER I

Naming Theories

1. Introduction

From the earliest known ship name, *Praise of the Two Lands*, given to a large cedarwood Egyptian vessel in the time of Sneferu about 2680 B.C., to the name of the latest vessel launched today, a thread of tradition in ship naming stretches unbroken through more than 4,500 years. To be sure, from some periods no names have survived, so it cannot be maintained that all major cultures in all periods have named ships. However, that epigraphical or other direct evidence is lacking is not conclusive, because the continuity of a strong tradition in nearly everything involving ships is well established. Thus it seems likely that the use of names, at least for large craft, has continued essentially uninterrupted from Sneferu's day and, indeed, from a still earlier time in prehistory, because pictorial evidence from about 4300 B.C.—over 1,500 years before Sneferu—shows Egyptians using riverine craft about fifty-five feet long, having a deckhouse, and propelled by numerous paddles.

2. Why Ships Have Names

Ships have names for four distinct reasons, reasons that in practice tend to be mixed in different combinations.

First, there is the religious reason, to invoke the favor of supernatural beings, always a compelling reason through all ages and apparently among all peoples.

Second, there is the sentimental reason, involving fancy, emotion, pride of ownership, or the feeling that a ship almost has a life of its own.

Third, there is the politico-economic reason, to flatter some individual, group, or nation in order to gain friendship, financial advantage, or military support; to develop national pride and unity; or to inspire group loyalty among individuals serving aboard in order that they will achieve and if necessary die together.

Finally—of prime importance—there is the simple reason that identification is necessary. It is necessary (1) to establish ownership and legal responsibility, (2) for convenience in private and official record keeping relating to the conduct of business, customs, taxation, and warfare, (3) to differentiate ships for the convenience of warriors, passengers, shippers, agents, and other countries, and (4) sometimes to gain renown or publicity in order to attract business by making a reputation for fast passages, luxury service, or other advantages.

3. Identification Methods

Apart from secondary psychological influences, a ship's name is above all a means of identification. Accordingly, in considering the development of ship names alternative means of distinguishing one ship from another should be examined.

The first alternative is identification by appearance—by size, shape, type, and color. For the really observant person at sea or on the waterfront appearance is frequently the first means of identification, particularly from a distance, though the name is required for confirmation. Identification of a ship in written records solely by its appearance would require such minute description as to be entirely impracticable. Nevertheless, because of the existence of ships of the same name and type, brief differentiating descriptions have at times been entered into records.

The second way to identify a ship is by its position, for example, position at a particular berth, linking that ship to whoever is associated with that berth. On an elementary basis, the position of a fishing craft drawn up on a beach identifies it as belonging to the fisherman who customarily uses that location.

This leads to a third identification method, which is the formalization of a mental association between vessel and owner or vessel and captain. This method is actually the same as naming the craft *John's Boat*.

So far, nothing has had to be added to the vessel solely to identify it. Appearance or position or both have sufficed and would suffice for a limited number of vessels among a limited number of informed persons. However, identification would be more positive and easier for more persons if a pattern of some sort were painted or carved on the structure, or if a design were painted on a sail. The added something might be a personal or impersonal symbol, a bow badge or figurehead, a design along the hull or at the stern, or a standard or ensign to indicate personal, group, or state ownership. By means of the symbol, as well as by identification of an owner, sooner or later a particularized ship name comes into use. One may well ask, however, which came first, the symbol that became a name or the name expressed as a symbol?

Finally, a ship may be identified by a name or a number or both, appearing at any of several locations on the vessel.

Another aspect of naming is not to make a ship known to others but simply to give it a name for convenience within a small group, as a family may apply a name to its motorcar, perhaps a somewhat affectionate "Lena" or more descriptively "The Clunker." Countless examples can also be cited of the personal naming of inanimate objects—bells, guns, swords, and houses. In particular, whenever danger is involved in the use of some object upon which reliance must be placed for individual or group preservation, there is a strong tendency to personify that object, for example, names on World War II airplanes that had to penetrate enemy heartlands under hazardous fire, names serving no purpose in an air force using identification numbers.

Of all the means of ship identification, for whatever purpose, only the name or the number is useful for written records. And the name alone is adequate for remembering, being not only a convenience but also a conduit of meaning and emotion.

4. Emotional Content

While not all ship names carry an emotional content, many do, as is obvious from an examination of ship lists or a look around a large harbor or yacht marina. Such emotional content may involve a person (hence many personal names, especially feminine) or a personification of the vessel (as feminine or with feminine qualities but often with vigorous masculine characteristics). It may refer to a sentiment about nature (flowers, trees, clouds). It may derive from a memory of childhood, a recollection from youth, an adult achievement, a religious experience, or a response to music or literature or war—in short, from whatever has left its mark upon an individual. Not always, of course, is the emotional content obvious to the outsider. Often, however, it is part of the common experience of mankind.

If we let the imagination wander, we may apprehend the nature of this aspect of the naming process. The name *Butterfly*, a very old name, is still used on ships. Perhaps somebody saw a ship's billowing sails as looking rather like a butterfly's wings. Perhaps a lonely young sailor returning from a long passage, eager for the sight of land, still somewhere over the horizon, the weather being fair and the wind gentle, sees a fragile butterfly settle on rail or rigging nearby. He marvels that so delicate a creature could stray so far from land and hopes that it like himself will reach shore again. This unexpected encounter with evanescent beauty is memorable, and should that sailor become a shipnamer and cast about for a name, he may remember the butterfly from his youth. Or a ship owner may remember having gone to sea on *Butterfly* or having received his first command on *Butterfly*, and in a measure relives his past by carrying on the old name.

Primrose (1538) and *Gillyflower* (1546) in an old ship list bring to mind flowers growing by a doorstep. Perhaps those sixteenth-century mariners chose names that reminded them of loved ones or of flowers in secret places they frequented as children. *Fairy Dell* was a nineteenth-century Scottish trading smack.[1]

Sea Flower, a favorite nineteenth-century Maine name, conveys the image of a ship's white sails blossoming on a blue field. The common name *Dolphin* recalls the welcome sight of these friendly creatures as they enjoy an underwater sleighride on the pressure wave at the bow. When I first saw *Tropic Bird* on a ship list, for a brig (1872) registered at the port of Eureka, California, it brought immediately to mind an encounter far offshore with one of these lonely fisher birds, which often permit approach within a few yards before taking wing. It was therefore easy to imagine some mariner's surprised delight in seeing this handsome, black-and-white, gull-sized, scarlet-billed bird with its two incredibly long, thin, up-curving feathers projecting an entire body length beyond the tail. These feathers suggested the old name *marlinspike bird*; its cry like a rattling whistle suggested the name *bosun bird*; and its plunge out of the sky into the sea suggested its Latin name after Phaethon, son of Apollo. Columbus reported this bird as *rabojunco*. *Tropic Bird* was also carried by an Oregon barkentine (1882), a New Bedford, Massachusetts, bark (1851), a New Bedford brig (1879), and is used today.

5. Naming Origins

Since the origins of ship naming are shrouded in prehistory, only tentative conclusions can be reached. Many elements in the naming process suggest different possible origins. Did the practice begin as a convenience in primitive commerce? Did it result from primitive minds' conceiving personality as existing in inanimate objects? How much name magic, how much religion, how much pure fancy were involved? Perhaps all these elements and others were operative—one more, another less; one dominant in one place, another somewhere else.

Although history provides some clues, others may be found in the observation of customs among peoples still at stages of cultural development that the Egyptians and others went through millenniums ago. James Hornell studied the customs of primitive fishermen on remote coasts of India and Ceylon and among certain Arabs and Malays.[1] Valuable insights were obtained about launching ceremonies, dedication to local deities, and worship at the bow. Surviving customs in more advanced areas of the world have also been studied and conclusions drawn regarding the more distant past, and, of course, archaeologists have unearthed evidence for interpretation by scholars. Still, much uncertainty remains.

Nevertheless, with the information available, an examination of known ship names from many periods to find a common thread linking them together through the ages suggests that *in a broad sense ship names originated as owner names.*

In this theory of ship name origination, the term *owner* is not limited to the private individual. In fact, it is unlikely that craft other than the smallest were privately owned until relatively late in cultural development. In the dim past, the owner might be the local god, the tribe, or the tribal chief; later, the city-state's god or gods or the regent king. Still later the owner might be the private person, a group, a corporation, or a great nation.

The tendency to identify ships by ownership has waxed and waned through history, from a single ship carrying the sign of a primitive divinity to the more than 200 tankers bearing the *Esso* and *Exxon* prefix today. Often ownership names persist along with different official names, even to the point—as with several ships of Columbus—where only the owner names were commonly used.

In many primitive communities, as well as in more advanced city-states and ancient nations, the real ruler was considered to be the god of each place (sometimes a pantheon of gods with one being dominant). The chief or king was only a vicar, expressing the will of the god. Everything belonged to the god, including the ships bearing his sign, whether intended for religious ceremonials, for transport, for trade, or for war. To the Hebrews (although they were not seafarers) this concept of divine rule meant that for centuries no king whatever should stand between them and God.

The king might become an owner in two ways. He might assume part of the god's divinity, usually an inevitable step, or his power might become so absolute that he owned whatever he pleased. Either as co-owner or owner, his name or his titles like those of the god became associated with state ships. This happened in Egypt, and vestiges of the practice may be seen in *Henri Grâce à Dieu* (1514),[2] in *Royal Charles* (1673),[3] and even today in *H.M.S.*

Privately owned vessels, it may be assumed from examples in later times, were often identified by owner, although no early names are known for these. Unless an owner has more than one ship (in which case his name tends to identify the line), his name serves best to convey essential information to those with whom he does business. It indicates his nationality; his family; his reputation for fair dealing, for caution at sea, and for fast service; and his policy in handling certain cargo or visiting certain ports. Among large merchant ships today, which belong usually to companies, the line name, not the ship name, may appear amidship on the hull in letters larger than man-size as an advertisement of ownership. During the long history of seafaring some private and some state-owned vessels have been identified by the names of their captains as quasi-owners; the owner may have found such identification a legal or an administrative convenience or may have wanted to boast about a captain with a good reputation or, by flattery, to keep a valuable man.

Surviving early ship names are by no means limited to owner names. The point is that such names have always existed and may have been the first names used. Owner names very early would have been supplemented by other names for state-owned vessels, perhaps because more names were required than were available from names of gods or goddesses or royal titles. The tendency to use private owner names (or family names) is strong when economic conditions permit one person or one family to hold sole or majority ownership and thus to display a reputation and pride of ownership; the tendency is less strong when vessels are owned in shares by a number of partners. A corporation, the modern form of shareholding, owns most large ships today, quite probably using "pattern" or "series" names to indicate ownership.

Further support for the ownership theory of ship naming comes from archaeological evidence. Along the banks of the Nile, archaeologists conclude, there were a string of small independent villages, each worshipping a local deity represented by a totem symbol, which also served as the clan or community symbol. It is reasonable to suppose, from what is known of primitive societies today, that prehistoric Egyptians applied these symbols to their watercraft in dedicating them to their gods. As trade developed among villages along the river, these symbols identified ships and in effect became ship names.

In time, with the development of communities and their grouping into the small kingdoms that eventually became dynastic Egypt, river commerce flourished with the employment of innumerable watercraft. God signs continued to be used on watercraft, but although Egypt had many gods, it had far more boats than gods, and confusion was bound to exist in keeping the voluminous records of the Egyptian bureaucracy. To differentiate royal craft and temple craft, various aspects of a god's name were probably used, as well as the names and titles of the divine pharaoh. Names having no connection with the gods or the ruler were also probably given to less important craft employed in carrying messages, transporting minor officials, ferrying citizens, and freighting stone or grain. This is not to imply that every little reed craft on the Nile had a name, nor even—since evidence is completely lacking—that private craft had names, apart from being identified in some way with owners. However, ample evidence does exist, as will be seen when Egyptian names are considered, that the Egyptians, consistent in their pragmatism, named many individual ships.

6. Name Magic and Secrecy

While the ownership theory of ship name origins seems to be the most plausible explanation, there are also other aspects to the matter. For example, man may have named ships as he named other things, especially those with which he felt a personal identification. Historical research has failed to discover any peoples lacking personal names. Very early, too, personal names were given to gods and to demons, who were believed to have a life of their own, as surely as the ram of the flock or the pet by the fireside, which also received personal names. Also long before maritime commerce developed, quasi-personal names were probably given by children to crude dolls and by men to other inanimate things, such as trustworthy weapons, star patterns, and maybe even watercraft that carried them safely.

Certainly, name magic has been involved at times in the naming process. To know the real name of a deity or a person or a thing was to gain power over it, as Adam gained power over the animals by naming them. Also through name magic the power inherent in the deity or thing could be used indirectly to ward off evil or accomplish good. The Egyptian through magical means learned the secret names of the gods, so that after death his spirit upon meeting a god could say, "I know your name," a knowledge that helped him obtain an afterlife with the gods.

This name magic, as the Bible shows, persisted in the Semitic world into a late period and in a limited way into the present. When Moses asked God his name, the reply came, "I am who I am," for God would not reveal His name. Among Semites a person's name corresponded to his essence. Among some Gypsies and Hindus name magic is influential today. In some Gypsy bands each member has a secret name, whispered into his ear at birth by his mother and repeated in the same manner at puberty, a name that not even the father knows. The individual is known to fellow Gypsies by his second, or baptismal, name and often to outsiders by yet a third name. Thus demons are denied power and police inquiries confounded. Among all classes of Hindus in India the superstition persists of giving opprobrious names to children born after the death of an earlier child in order to fool demons into thinking that a boy called "Fool," "Beggar," or "Worm" or a girl called "Louse," "Lame," or "Nit" was not worth noticing. Goethe in his autobiography characterized a name as a "veritable skin grown" on a man "which can be mutilated only with injury to the man himself."

Not only persons but also some cities had secret names. Rome's was Valentia. It is not impossible that ships at times had secret names. Although this thought is advanced very tentatively indeed, it could explain why ship names do not occur in some early records. Secret names for ships, if they existed, very likely would have been used, as in the case of personal secret names, together with nonsecret convenience names.

Some investigators have thought that ships acquired personality because of the ancient belief that hamadryads or other wood creatures were a vital part of trees and therefore that something of the wood spirits remained in the ship's timbers. This supposition would assume personality in anything made of wood and is consequently not convincing. It is much more likely that the conception that a god's spirit existed in ships originated in another way. In light of the belief of ancient peoples that different places belonged to different gods, it would have been inconsistent for the Egyptians to take cedar from Byblos without first placating the god of that area by erecting a temple and honoring him there. To do otherwise would have been to invite disaster at sea, for some vestige of ownership by the god remained in the cedar, even when taken from his country. This concept also fits the ownership theory of naming, although it is not known that Egypt named ships after the Byblos baal. Another way for a presiding spirit—of a deity, a brave warrior, a strong animal, or a sea-conquering shark—to enter into a ship, particularly at the bow area, would be through a sacrificial launching ritual; for a symbol, particularly a statue, was not a mere representation but an actual depository of an essence.

However, speculation about religious customs, about what persons really believe, is hazardous. Even with primitive peoples of today there are barriers of culture and language. Did the ancients really believe that a spirit actually resided in the bow of a ship? Perhaps some only believed that by dedicating the bow they were reminding a supernatural power, wherever it existed, to watch over the vessel. It is even possible that figures presumed to have been religious in nature really had some other function, such as to intimidate subject peoples and warn possible enemies. Although some Egyptian ship figures did depict gods, certain victorious pharaohs sailing up the Nile displayed the bodies of captured kings bound to the bow. Royal prows in a later period had carvings representing bound Semite and African enemies, just as the carving on pharaoh's footstool showed a recumbent foreign subject.

In connection with the concept of a ship's having a personality apart from that of her owner or master, it is interesting that today this concept somewhat altered is embodied in maritime law, as it was in medieval times. It is illustrated by this quotation from a United States Supreme Court decision of 1902:

A ship is born when she is launched, and lives so long as her identity is preserved. Prior to her launching she is a mere congeries of wood and iron—an ordinary piece of personal property—as distinctly a land structure as a house, and subject only to mechanics liens created by a state law and enforceable in the state courts. In the baptism of launching she receives her name, and from the moment her keel touches the water she is transformed, and becomes a subject of admiralty jurisdiction. She acquires a personality of her own; becomes competent to contract, and is individually liable for obligations, upon which she may sue in the name of her owner, and be sued in her own name. Her owner's agents may not be her agents, and her agents may not be her owner's agents. She is capable, too, of committing a tort, and is responsible in damages therefor. She may also become a quasi bankrupt; may be sold for the payment of her debts, and thereby receive a complete discharge from all prior liens, with liberty to begin a new life, contract further obligations, and perhaps be subjected to a second sale. Tucker v. Alexandroff, 183 U.S. 424, 438.[1]

CHAPTER II

Naming Practices

7. Naming Ceremonies

THE naming of a child is often confirmed at a christening or other ritual, an event of considerable ceremony. Ceremonies at the launching of a ship predate the Christian era. An Assyrian tablet of 2100 B.C., in recounting the completion of a ship, includes the king's words: "To the gods I caused oxen to be sacrificed." The early Greeks used wine at the launching ceremony, and in modern Greece vestiges of this rite survive, when the bow is decorated with the nonbloody sacrifice of flowers, and when, as the ship hits the water, the captain takes a sip of wine and pours the rest on deck. The Turks sacrificed sheep as a vessel slid into the water, the flesh being given to the poor. Ancient Norsemen practiced roller-reddening, the attaching of a human victim to the launching rollers. Human blood was shed in Tahiti when a new canoe was launched. Sacrifices have been offered at launchings for thousands of years and throughout the world.

The earliest record of blessing an English ship dates from about 1390 when the custom was already old. In eighteenth-century France the launching and naming resembled a baptism, with sponsors or godparents, sometimes a boy and a girl, and with a priest sprinkling blessed water. In most Protestant lands the Reformation abolished the religious observance, except perhaps for a prayer by a clergyman or sovereign, but the pagan practice of libation of wine was revived. While champagne is the customary libation today, *Constitution* was christened in 1797 with a bottle of choice old Madeira. Admiral David Farragut's Civil War flagship, the steam sloop *Hartford* (1858), received her name when one young woman broke a bottle of Hartford spring water, another a bottle of Connecticut River water, and an officer a bottle of Atlantic seawater.[1]

The importance of the naming ceremony is illustrated—in its absence—by the indifference to the launching in 1966 of a frigate ordered by a regime in Ghana subsequently overthrown. The Clyde-side builders did not know whether the new regime would honor the contract; hence the warship slid into the water without a name, and, significantly, not even the shipyard workers gathered round to witness the event.[2]

8. Good Names

Regardless of religious customs, modern man is quite aware that in personifying a ship he is nevertheless actually dealing with an inanimate thing, although something *seeming* to have certain lifelike qualities, something to which he entrusts his very life, something worthy of a personal name.

A modern expression of this personifying tendency is found in *The Sea and the Jungle* where H. M. Tomlinson referred to the freighter *Capella*: "I learned why a ship has a name. It is for the same reason that you or I have names. She has happenings according to her own weird. She shows perversities and virtues her parents never dreamed into the plans they laid for her." Or as Joseph Conrad succinctly observed, ships are "not exactly what we make them" but "have their own nature." Hilaire Belloc expressed another aspect of the same idea when he remarked that no vessel will do her best unless sufficiently flattered.

Respect for the ship follows from this attitude. Such respect would be stronger among seagoing sailors than among rivermen, stronger among those aboard small craft than among those on modern behemoths. Perhaps nobody who has never actually confronted the basic hostility of the sea can comprehend the feeling of the mariner for the craft that carries him, often wet and weary and gale lashed, through to what the Greek poet called "the sweet homecoming won in spite of the sea." Conrad said that the seadog's profanity, provoked by hardships of the sea, rarely went so far as to touch his ship; and if occasionally it did, it was only lightly, "as a hand may, without sin, be laid in the way of kindness on a woman."[1] In time of danger, in this century, more than one captain has been heard talking to his ship, urging her to rise to the next great sea or to come about safely.

Respect for the ship requires the bestowal of a good name, the religious name being first and foremost in that category through the ages. Danger at sea must be largely responsible for the powerful impulse of mariners to petition supernatural help, most pronounced when ships were small and men more aware of what Herman Melville called the "tiger heart" panting beneath the frequently "tranquil beauty and brilliancy of the ocean's skin." Nobody with any wide experience loves the sea, not really; love for the sea is a fiction of poets. What the mariner loves is his illusion of mastery over an alien element, the exercise of his skill in surviving. He loves memorable days at sea, but not the sea itself, which is brooding and treacherous. So there have always been religious ship names, and occasionally even the outright plea, such as *God Save Her* in early seventeenth-century England.[2] Sometimes, consciously or otherwise, men apparently have attempted to foil the heartless sea by selecting names suggesting strength, safety, and survival, such names as *Determined, Resolute, Intrepid,* and *Reliant.* The term *maru* on Japanese ships gives every one a good name. (See section on "Maru.")

But good names are not limited to petitions for survival against the perils of the deep. They include just about everything that is good in life, from a field flower such as *Daisy* to an abstraction such as *World Justice.* Good names may refer to a ship's fine handling qualities, her turn of speed, her carrying ability, her earning power. They inform, plead, rebuke, threaten, honor, and inspire. They include names of places, incidents, exploits, hopes; names of love, friendship, trust, confidence, determination. Good names may be images, metaphors, or symbols conveying overtones of meaning quite impossible to interpret.

Victory is an excellent example of a good name for a warship and was used by Greeks and Romans, long before Nelson's day. Both *Dainty* and the sixteenth-century Portuguese treasure ship she captured, *Madre de Dios,* had good names. *Spray,* the first craft to be sailed single-handed around the world, has a namesake in nearly every yacht harbor. *Olympic Flame* (1950), Liberian tanker; *Bluebird* (1968), Japanese bulk carrier; and *Saga Sky* (1965), Norwegian tanker—all bear good names. And so does the very prosaic *Joseph H. Thompson* (1944), freighter of Wilmington, Delaware.

A good name ideally should be easy to remember, easy to spell, easy to pronounce, harmonious in sound, and agreeable in meaning. However, a perusal of any register or a look around any harbor will disclose good names that fail entirely to meet these standards. They are good, nevertheless, because they meet certain canons that, with few exceptions, are universal in ship nomenclature. These canons include respect for the vessel, a sense of fitness, and often a feeling for tradition.

Respect for the vessel precludes such a name as *Rake's Delight,* though perhaps it suited a slaver sailing out of Sunbury, Georgia, in 1776.[3] On the other hand, plain *Delight,* one of the ships under Sir Francis Drake and Sir John Hawkins in 1595, had a name as fit as any. The name may be a commonplace *Mary* or an imaginative *Grand Mistress*; both have integrity and reflect the sober hope, the implied trust, even the love of real seamen. A sense of fitness is seen in *Flying Cloud* for a clipper, in *Defiance* for a warship, and in *Discovery* for a ship of exploration.

As for tradition, a ship can make her own, but often names from the past are carried on, as was true, in an outstanding example, of the series of Venetian galleys, each named *Bucentaur*, the first built in 1311 and the last in 1728, and all used in the Espousal of the Sea ceremony.[4] The name of this golden galley is believed to have derived from *Bucintoro*, which in turn came from *buzino d'oro*, "bark of gold." Many ancient names, such as those of pagan gods, with their original significance lost in transfer to a different culture, remain good names because of tradition.

Where the canons of nomenclature—respect, fitness, tradition—are followed, ship names are likely to inspire loyalty, pride, and often bravery among those serving aboard. Many a warship's proud name has meant the difference between defeat and victory in battle. The inspired name has always been a unifying device in war, but especially on ships. Scholars sometimes find it hard to distinguish between the names of ancient Egyptian ships and regiments. Certain ship names like certain regiment names acquire an aura of traditional glory. One American unit, the First Armored Division, even carries the nickname of a famous warship, "Old Ironsides." Because a ship keeps men in close association for long periods, the good name is even more important for sailors than for soldiers.

CHAPTER III

Ancient Ships

9. Egypt

IF THE Egyptians were not the first to use ship names, at least they were the first known, because they thought in terms of eternity and left stone-carved inscriptions detailing events in the lives of prominent men who sometimes had been associated with ships.

The role of the Nile in Egypt's development can hardly be overemphasized. This river flowed slowly enough for easy passage upstream under oar or sail. From the sea to the First Cataract was about 500 miles, and at different times there were canals around that cataract and even branching off the Nile to the Red Sea. All types of watercraft abounded, from small sporting boats for hunting waterfowl and hippopotamuses to Nile-based fleets capable of controlling the Mediterranean. So vital were watercraft to the Egyptians that many tomb inscriptions characterize a man without a boat as being among the unfortunate, along with the orphan and the naked.[1] The nobleman traveled with servants in his "yacht," accompanied by an eight-oared commissary boat to prepare his meals. Whole fleets of transports carried taxes-in-kind and tribute to the royal treasury. An assistant treasurer in the Theban nome built sixty ships for the commerce of his area alone. More than one nobleman affirmed in his tomb inscription that he "gave bread to the hungry, water to the thirsty, clothing to the naked, and a ferry-boat to the boatless," these being good works to impress the gods.[2] So ingrained in Egyptian thinking were ships and the Nile that Queen Hatshepsut was termed the "bow-cable of the South" and the "stern-cable of the North."[3]

These figures of speech seem to refer to a tendency for Egypt, a strip-nation along the Nile, to snap apart politically. Hence *Praise of the Two Lands* is not only the earliest ship name known but also the first suggesting political overtones.[4] Like several later Egyptian names it stressed unity between North and South, in a manner not unlike the naming of a British ship *Union* when the union of Scotland with England occurred.

Praise of the Two Lands, about 167 feet long, was one of two of that size built about 2680 B.C., in the first or second year of Sneferu's reign, when he also built sixty "sixteen-barges." Quite likely these were mostly made from the forty shiploads of cedar Sneferu imported in Egyptian bottoms from Lebanon. The aforementioned early ship name exhibits several other aspects of naming, apart from the obvious one of identification. Very likely it was the title of a god, possibly Re, or referred not only to the god but also to his divine pharaonic deputy, honoring them both. At the same time, it was doubtless a plea for divine protection for the ship. Finally, this worthy name indicated national pride. In fact all Egyptian ships known about had worthy names—even *Cow* in the time of Tuthmosis III (1504–1450 B.C.), for besides representing the goddess Hathor the cow was considered a very beautiful animal.[5]

Translations of Egyptian names have been taken from archaeological journals or historical works, but most have been newly translated by Dr. John B. Callender. In this century scholars have found meaning in Egyptian names previously not understood, while other names previously incorrectly or literally translated have been given different meanings. Some known ship names still yield no sense at all. The works of Wilhelm Spiegelberg,[6] James H. Breasted,[7] Torgny Säve-Söderbergh,[8] and W. M. F. Petrie[9] are the principal sources used.

Another early ship was *Mighty Is Isesi*, a great Nile towboat near the end of the Fifth Dynasty (2565–2420 B.C.), when Dedkere-Isesi was pharaoh.[10] Obviously, the name honored the ruler, who lived about the middle of a remarkable 500-year period when Egyptian art and mechanics flowered. Pharaoh was indeed mighty.

The next dated name is that of a god's barge, *Appearing in Truth, the Lord of Abydos*, referring to Osiris, in the Twelfth Dynasty (1991–1786 B.C.).[11] This name is known because a priestly actor, proud of having impersonated the son of Osiris in funerary rites for the god, during a festival utilizing the barge, had the account engraved on a stela found at Abydos.

The fullest naval records are from the Eighteenth Dynasty (1570–1349 B.C.), in the Late Bronze Age, when Egypt created an empire extending from northern Syria and the upper Euphrates to the Fourth Cataract of the Nile. Two facts influenced ship names in the Eighteenth and Nineteenth Dynasties: (1) the pharaohs were concerned not only with ruling foreigners but also with keeping the feudal nobles at home under control, and (2) Amon became the national deity, and his priesthood at Thebes became extremely powerful. Thus most known ship names had religious and royal propaganda value.

The names of four ships are known from the reign of Ahmose I (1570–1545 B.C.), first ruler of the New Kingdom. Three were warships. The names of such ships usually appear in conjunction with the names of captains, either in official records or on tomb inscriptions. As the navy was not distinct from the army, ship names resembled regimental names. One warship was the *Northern*.[12] Another was *Shining in Memphis*, perhaps shining with decorations of gold or electrum, but more probably an allusion to pharaoh, or possibly to Ptah, who in Memphite theology was creator of the universe.[13] The name of the third warship illustrates the progress made since Spiegelberg termed it *The Sacrificial Animal* and Breasted *The Offering*; Säve-Söderbergh translated it as *The Wild Bull* because it is now known that *wild bull* was a metaphorical name for pharaoh.[14] (*Lion of Judah*, a 1966 Ethiopian freighter, has exactly the same type of metaphorical name as *The Wild Bull*, although separated in time by over 2,500 years.)[15] Ahmose, son of Ebana, who became chief of the sailors, sailed on all three of the foregoing Egyptian ships, according to his tomb biography. The fourth ship known from the time of Ahmose I was *Amon Re in the Sacred Barge*, a royal vessel of cedar, used also to carry a statue of Amon in festivals arranged by his powerful priests.[16]

This last ship name occurs again, four pharaohs later, in the time of Tuthmosis III; but then the barge was either new or extensively rebuilt, as is known from the tomb of the man who supervised the work. He recorded that it was "wrought with gold" and that "it illuminated the Two Lands with its rays." Once again, the barge of Amon-Re was either rebuilt or replaced by Tuthmosis IV (1423–1410 B.C.), and the name reappears also in later reigns. This is the first recorded instance of a name's being carried by successive ceremonial vessels, for about 500 years as compared with slightly over 400 years for the ornate Venetian craft *Bucentaur*. That the Amon-Re barge was not only for ceremony, however, is shown by a record stating that Tuthmosis III used it to transport wives and children of vanquished enemies.

In the time of Amenhotep (1410–1372 B.C.) the Amon-Re barge was made large with "new cedar" dragged over mountains by "the princes of all countries." In words from the time: "It was made very wide and large, there is no instance of doing the like. It is adorned with silver, wrought with gold throughout, the great shrine is of electrum so that it fills the land with its brightness; they bear great crowns, whose serpents twine along its two sides; they exercise protection behind them." Ramesses III (1195–1164) built a cedar barge of Amon nearly 224 feet long, "overlaid with fine gold to the waterline." Under this ruler the Temple of Amon became so powerful that its inventory listed eighty-three ships.

The last mention of the god's barge comes from Egypt's declining period, about 1075 B.C., when Wenamon, agent of Amon's high priest, suffered shipwreck, robbery, and insults before finally obtaining cedar from Lebanon for yet another in the series of vessels.

Other ships in the Eighteenth Dynasty included a royal ship of Tuthmosis III called *Star of the Two Lands* (just as ships today may be called *Star of* this or that place).[17] He also had two vessels, probably warships, called *Menkheperre Is the Smiter of Syria*, Menkheperre being Tuthmosis III, and *Loved by Amon*, a pharaonic title.[18] In his reign there were also *The Stable* (perhaps a horse transport)[19] and the previously mentioned *Cow*.

The next ruler, Amenhotep II (1450–1423 b.c.), also found it expedient to stress the unity of Egypt. He had ships called *Amenhotep II Unites Both Lands, Amenhotep II Is Established on the Throne*, and *Appearing in Truth*.[20] His successor, Tuthmosis IV, had another *Loved by Amon*, while his successor, Amenhotep III, had an *Appearing in Truth* and *Aton Gleams*.[21] The latter sailed on a lake dug for the queen. The name could be translated "Shining Sun Disc" and referred to the sun god that this pharaoh's son attempted to have replace all the deities of Egypt.

Sety I (1313–1301 b.c.) had vessels called *Life, Prosperity, and Health Have Come into Being in Egypt* (a long name, indeed, although only five words in ancient Egyptian writing), *Loved by Amon, Aton Gleams*, and *Appearing in Opet*.[22] Opet was the main feast of Amon at Luxor. Ramesses II called one of his ships *Ramesses II, Pacifier of Aton*,[23] perhaps indicating a tolerance of the worship of Aton following the violent reaction to Aton-worship in the previous half century.

Other vessels of the Eighteenth and perhaps the Nineteenth Dynasties, but not more precisely dated, included *Amon, Loved by Re, Star in Memphis, Victorious, Master of Egypt, Strong Ruler, Excelling in Beauty* and *Ptah at the Bow*.[24] The last would have had an effigy of the god of craftsmen, wrapped as a mummy and holding a scepter at the breast; this figure alone could have conveyed the name.

The use of effigy raises the question of whether hieroglyphic names or only symbols appeared on Egyptian ships. We cannot be sure. Probably either or both were used at different times. Certainly, many of the ship names seem too complex by far for a simple symbol. W. M. F. Petrie translated a Theban ostrakon, undated but probably from the Eighteenth Dynasty, giving the names and stone-block loads of about two dozen vessels. These included *Sword, Turnabout, Beloved, Mighty, Harvest, Feast, Bull, Council, Year, White, Flourishing, Thebes Shines*, and *Remainder*. Petrie observed that "nearly all these words are single signs which could be set up as a figurehead or painted large upon the bows."[25]

Since other tallies of this type transcribed by Spiegelberg list the names of owners rather than the names of vessels, and since Petrie concluded from the writing on the Theban ostrakon that the scribe was not a regular one, some substitute scribe may have departed unwittingly from custom

in tallying stones or perchance was too lazy to get up from his shady van-
tage point to go learn the owners' names, especially since a single sign
was possibly easier to put on stone than an owner's name. This ostrakon
provides a telling argument whenever it is asserted that ships, for whatever ancient land, must have lacked names if they are known to us only
through ownership.

   In this regard, a papyrus receipt of 252 B.C., long after ship names were
certainly common throughout the Mediterranean world, given by an
Egyptian captain, for barley loaded for Alexandria, shows that the captain himself identified the vessel for legal purposes by the names of its
owners, captain, and pilot: "Dionysius, boat captain, acknowledges that
he has embarked upon the transport of Xenodocus and Alexander, of
which Ekteuris son of Pasis, of Memphis, is pilot, through Nechthembes
the agent of the royal scribes, for conveyance to Alexandria to the royal
granary, with a sample, 4800 artabae of barley."[26]

10. Mesopotamia

Information about the use of ship names by the ancient Mesopotamian
peoples is somewhat obscure, despite extensive water commerce on canals
and on the Tigris, the Euphrates, and the Persian Gulf. Armas Salonen
listed about three dozen types of Mesopotamian watercraft, from simple
rafts supported by inflated animal skins to seagoing vessels such as those
the Merchants of Ur, about 1900 B.C., sent regularly down the gulf to the
free port on the island known today as Bahrein.[1] Mesopotamian craft
used in commerce varied in capacity, by today's measurement, from less
than one registered ton to slightly over twenty-eight tons. Hammurabi
had 7,200 logs, 300 to a ship, brought down river to Babylon. Ships in
large numbers were owned by rulers, by temples, and by individuals.
Officials, priests, tax collectors, investors, merchants, agents, stevedores,
ferrymen, and others were all involved with shipping, as the surviving
law codes and commercial records spell out in detail.

   Yet none of the clay tablets so far published (thousands remain to be
deciphered) mention commercial craft by name. That individual names
do not appear only suggests that the recording of such names, if they existed, was not considered necessary. Experience in archaeology repeatedly
shows how misleading arguments *ex silentio* can be. What was important for the record was the boat's capacity in *gur* as well as the name of
the owner or captain who had direct legal and financial responsibility.
Grain receipts from Ur of about 2000 B.C. mention the "ship of Lu-gi-

anna," the "ship of Sur-dun," and many others.² If these craft did not have names as we know them, certainly the extent of commerce suggests they required differentiation by emblem or other means.

In a few instances, however, terms were applied to ships of the gods that several scholars consider to be specific names. Usually such gods' ships were simply called "Enlil's ship" or "Enki's ship," for example, and perhaps were processional vessels or ships operated commercially by temples of the particular gods. Thus, whether "Enki's ship" may be considered a specific name or a class name depends upon whether one or more existed in a particular city at the same time, that is, whether reference is to a single craft used in religious ceremonies or to one of a number of temple commercial carriers.

However, there is another type of name. In a few cases such a name appears as *Deer of the Ocean*, an Enki ship. Salonen, an authority on Babylonian watercraft, translated it as *"Ozeanssteinbock"* ("Ocean Stonebuck"). *Absu*, the term in the original for ocean, probably refers to the primordial waters around and under the earth, or indirectly to such waters particularized in some sacred lagoon, such as that at ancient Eridu on the Persian Gulf where the temple to Enki originally stood, or to some symbolic pool of water in a temple. The word for deer could also be translated as "stag" or "wild goat." Eric Burrows studied this name and concluded it was not, as applied to the vessel, a mere title of the god but rather a specific ship name.³ He called it *Wild Goat of the Absu* and theorized it may have had a goat's head on the prow. Burrows also cited what he termed "another ship name," *Ship of the Restless Absu*, translated elsewhere as *Ship of the Spirit Arising from the Pool of the Depths*.⁴ This ship was dedicated to the god Ningirsu by Gudea, who ruled Lagash at a time variously dated between 2600 and 2200 B.C. Lagash was situated on a major canal linking the Tigris and the Euphrates. The famous statue of Gudea is in the Louvre.

Dr. Giorgio Buccellati translated from the Akkadian, as cited by Salonen, the following terms, which might be specific ship names: *Pure Wild Cow, Great Cow, Ship That Does Not Land* [?], *Great Storm*, and *He Does Not Know a Roof*.

Pure Wild Cow was a ship of Bau, goddess of medicine, whose symbol apparently was a dog and not a cow. *Great Cow* symbolized the moon god Enzu, probably because up-curving cow's horns resembled both the horns of the crescent moon and the upturned ends of the ship. *Moon-ship* appears to have been a generic term for this type. Perhaps *Pure Wild Cow* also had such a shape. *Ship That Does Not Land* was another crescent-shaped moon-god ship from Ur; the name may have referred to how the craft was used ceremonially or to some aspect of moon-god mythology. *Great Storm* referred to Adad, god of storms. *He Does Not Know a Roof*, might mean "without a deck" or "without a deckhouse"; or more literally it might have referred to the god himself, in the sense that Enlil could not be contained beneath a roof. It might even have had a meaning similar to that in the New Testament passage referring to the Son of Man as having "no place to lay his head."

It has been suggested that ship names were not used by Mesopotamian people because the Marsh Arabs of today, occupying the silted-up delta area of the Euphrates, do not name their boats. Some of these small craft have upturned ends like the ancient moon-ships, ends that apparently serve to penetrate and part the high reeds of the marsh. These Arab boats are all quite small and are seldom employed on the large bodies of water except in skirting the edges. They are long, narrow, and flatbottomed with a shallow freeboard and are not large enough to handle the cargos of grain, copper ingots, and other items of ancient Babylonia's well-developed water commerce, though they may well resemble small craft used primarily for transportation, fishing, or fowling on the placid water areas of Babylonia. These modern craft need no names for identification because the Arabs of the sparsely settled region recognize at a glance the boats in their limited area and can often tell who built them.[5]

In conclusion, it would seem that some ancient Babylonian ships acquired names, if not by official intention, then by popular usage. If some were named, it is possible that the practice was generally observed. It also seems probable that the Assyrians, who carried on the watercraft activity of earlier Babylonia, also carried on and further developed the name usage.

11. Other East Mediterranean Peoples

What of the Hittites, who, according to Assyrian records, "cleverly built mighty ships" and used so much timber as to "make tall trees in the forests a rarity"? And what of all the "kings who live on the sea coast, who travel by boat instead of by chariot, who harness oars instead of horses"?[1] What of the Minoans, the Mycenaeans, the Phoenicians? Unfortunately, we have no name records.

Since the Egyptians used ship names, and since Egypt during her long empire period often dominated much of the eastern Mediterranean world militarily and always exerted a marked commercial and cultural influence, it is plausible that ship names were also used by other seafaring peoples. If so, the evidence is missing.

A cuneiform tablet from Ugarit dating from the fifteenth century B.C. enumerates the complements of three warships, each with eighty to ninety men.[2] First, each captain is named, then the provenance of his warriors, and lastly the numbers. Each complement is identified as "Host of the ship of Ben Ksan," and so on, for each captain. Now "ship of Ben Ksan" is a specific name, applied to one ship, though perhaps not a permanent name unless the captain was also the owner.

12. Greece

With the Greeks of the fifth century B.C., we come to a people known to have used written ship names, many of which translate into names seen today in any harbor or marina. Archaeologists believe the Minoans, earlier in the Greek world, used oared vessels seventy-five to one-hundred feet in length, but as for names, if any, scholars are still at work on Minoan and Mycenaean inscriptions in Linear A and B. This writing disappeared from the Greek world about 1200 B.C., and four centuries of cultural darkness apparently ensued. Subsequently, between the introduction of alphabetic writing about the eighth century and the period of Themistocles in the fifth century, it would seem that written ship names came into common use in Greece. Pindar, who died about the middle of the fifth century, cited *Argo* as Jason's ship, and the argument goes on as to whether this was an actual name of an actual ship named for an actual builder called Argus. Lionel Casson seems to think *Argo* (perhaps meaning *Swift*) truly existed as a fifty-oar galley used on a memorable Black Sea expedition.[1]

Possibly, as may have been true in Egypt, clan or "town" symbols were first used in the prehistoric period to identify Aegean ships. Such symbols did appear on shields and sometimes on coins—for instance, a bull's head or a chariot wheel. It is likewise possible that colors, with or without symbols, were used. The poets mentioned "red-prowed" and "blue-prowed" ships. Such prow colors—especially red to symbolize blood—may have indicated ritual dedication to a deity and, as such, nationality. An Etruscan tomb fresco at Tarquinia from perhaps the ninth century B.C. shows a fishing boat with a blue bow, the blue separated from the rest of the hull by slanting yellow and black bands. Perhaps the blue denoted nationality and the other colors the particular owner. In any event, probably the use of generalized symbols or colors was followed by more precise identification, with nationality still indicated by symbol, statue, color, standard, or a combination, and with something carved or painted to indicate the name. Cecil Torr discusses name symbolism on ancient

ships even as late at A.D. 200.[2] J. S. Morrison also deals with means of
identification on early Greek oared ships.

Whatever the sequence of development, the need for specific ship
names to avoid confusion is clearly shown by the decree of Themistocles,
480 B.C., setting forth preparations for dispatching about 200 galleys to
meet the Persian fleet at Salamis. As paraphrased by Morrison, the Athenian leader ordered that "the names of the trieres and of the trierarchs
and of the petty officers should head the list of each company so that each
company should know on which trieres to embark."[3] Although no
names of the galleys participating in the famous battle have been identified, inscription fragments from the last half of the same century identify
about a dozen warships that might have participated in the Samian War
(440–439 B.C.) or the Sicilian Expedition (415–413 B.C.).[4] Some names are
incomplete, others obscure; several are names of Attic tribes; one is the
name of an Egyptian port. Another is a feminine proper name *Eorte*, suggesting that the ship was a "feast to the eyes" or referring to some feast or
festival. The seafaring custom of perpetuating names makes it probable
that some of the galleys at Salamis bore names included in the large number from the fourth century B.C., over 260 names in all, that were inscribed
on marble as an inventory at the Athenian shipyard at Piraeus. From
these names, which may be found in *Corpus inscriptionum Graecarum*,
a generous sampling will be included here.[5]

Georges Gustave-Toudouze regarded these inscription names as ex-
alting the cult of the eternally feminine, as showing the attitude of the
Hellenic sea people, for whom the galley was a living feminine thing.[6] A
small selection would perhaps support this impression. It is true that the
names are largely feminine in gender, and it is also true that Greek watercraft words are feminine (as they are also in Akkadian and Latin and in
some instances in ancient Egyptian and in several modern European lan-
guages). On the whole, however, the names themselves do not suggest
that the attitude of the old Greeks was substantially different from that
of modern English-speaking men.

This fact is evident from a search for the Greek names in *British Warship Names* (*BWN*) and in *Merchant Vessels of the United States, 1968*
(*MVUS68*).[7, 8] The first source conveniently covers several centuries in
listing warships, Greek galleys being warships. Whenever a tally from
BWN is cited, the total includes all entries under a given name, although
there can be only one ship (or none) with a given name at a time. The
second source, *MVUS68*, offers a wide and representative cross section:
large vessels, smaller commercial craft, and yachts over five tons. The
yacht entries are not disproportionate since only an estimated one and

one-half percent of United States yachts are documented. Smaller craft should be included because the Greek galleys were relatively small. Ship size definitely affects a mariner's attitude both toward his ship and toward the sea and hence affects name choice.

The numerals in parentheses after each of the following Greek names at Piraeus indicate the number of entries in one or both of the aforementioned modern ship lists. As will be evident repeatedly in pages to follow, certain names and name types tend to run through Western history.

Angels (4, *Angel*), *Artemis* (1), *Audacious* (7), *Beautiful Stranger* (1, *Strange Girl*), *Beloved* (7, *Sweetheart*), *Best of All* (3, *Best Ever*), *Breeze* (1), *Charming* (4, *Charmer*), *Commander* (24), *Dawn* (33), *Democracy* (3, *Republic*), *Easy* (2), *Euphrosine* (1), *Europa* (5), *Excellence* (3, *Excellent*), *Famous* (13, *Fame*), *Friendliness* (16, *Friendship*), *Glory* (11), *Good Luck* (3), *Health* (1), *Huntress* (11), *Javelin* (2), *Joy* (17), *Kingfisher* (47), *Liberty* (24), *Fury* (20), *Merrily* (1), *Morning Star* (35), *Nereid* (16), *Pandora* (23), *Peace* (3), *Victory* (39), *Winged* (2, *Wings*), *Young Lady* (1)

Doubtless there would be numerous additional instances of modern duplication of the Piraeus names if apt synonyms were used for the following galley names as translated from the Greek:

Auspicious, Beautiful to Behold, Blameless, Comely, Competent, Darling, Deliverance, Flattery, Frivolous, Happiness, Help, Humility, Irreproachable, Lamp, Newest, Power, Safe Passage, Sufficiency, Virtuous, War Spirit.

More unusual are such Piraeus names as *Axwinke* (*Deserving Victory*), *Bather* (that is, a feminine one), *Cleostrate* (*War Glory*), *Order of Battle, Youth* (that is, a male teenager), *Through the Salty Sea*, and *Trophy* (perhaps *Prize*).

Most of the foregoing names, with numerous others found at Piraeus, had too many explicit and implicit meanings to have been indicated on ships only symbolically, although it must not be overlooked that certain abstractions could be personified by minor divinities, and that the ancients in portraying these differentiated them sometimes in subtle ways, as by hand position, body stance, garb, or accompanying object. Thus some abstract names could have been conveyed symbolically. In many cases, however, there could have been no connection between name and emblematic features, so that in such cases the name, if displayed on a ship at all, must have been printed on the structure or upon some standard.

From later centuries in Greece only a few ship names are known. One was *Lion Carrier* (*Leontophorus*), the supergalley, which may have been a giant catamaran, built at Heraclea on the Black Sea and used about 287

B.C. by Lysimachus as the principal unit of his fleet in expelling Demetrius I from Macedonia.[9] Another was *Isthmia*, in which about twenty years later the son of Demetrius, Antigonus Gonatas, won the Battle of Kos.[10]

13. Rome

Considering all we know about Roman civilization, it seems surprising how few ship names have survived in literary works; however, most historical accounts have been lost, and in those remaining the authors apparently did not consider such details important. Herodotus mentioned no ship by name in his account of the victory at Salamis; yet each Greek ship there is known to have had a specific name. Likewise 400 years later Plutarch cited no ship at Actium.

One possibly authentic source for early Roman ship names (and Carthaginian as well) is the heroic poem *Punica*, written in his old age by Silius Italicus, who was born about A.D. 25 and served as proconsul of Asia.[1] In book 14 there is a stirring account of a naval engagement off Sicily, supposedly having occurred near the end of Rome's three-year siege of Syracuse, during the Second Punic War, 218–201 B.C. In this account, *Chimaera* from Aeolia sank the Roman turret-ship *Nessus. Perseus* commanded by Tiberinus sank *Io*, which carried the Carthaginian Crantor. The poet perhaps described identifying emblems or decorations when he wrote:

Among the burning ships was *Cyane*, well known to those waters, and the winged *Siren*; *Europa*, too, who rode on the back of Jove disguised as a snow-white bull, and grasped one horn as she moved across the water; the watery *Nereid*, with floating hair, who drove a floating dolphin over the deep with dripping rein; the sea-traversing *Python* was burnt, and the horn-crowned *Ammon*, and the vessel that bore the likeness of Tyrian *Dido* and was propelled by six banks of oars.

Ammon was the Phoenician god, derived from the Egyptian Amon, and was represented bearded with ram's horns. Dido reputedly founded Carthage and was deified. Ships making shore included *Anapus* (river in Sicily) and *Pegasus*. Those taken as prizes included "that which bore the likeness of *Libya*," along with *Triton, Etna,* and *Sidon.* The nationality of several ships is not clear, perhaps because some belonged to Carthaginian allies or because Silius himself was unclear.

Did the foregoing ships really exist? No one can say for certain. Following closely the works of historians and geographers, Silius reported facts, ideas, and true incidents and exercised a minimum of poetic license. John Nichol, from studying sources available to the poet, decided that the sea fight was probably imaginary.[2] That conclusion is curious, however; Nichol apparently based it on the absence of the account in Livy, whereas elsewhere he concluded that, while Livy was an important authority for the poet, "he was never used alone and certainly was not preferred" to the numerous other historians then extant. Furthermore, Nichol showed how careful the poet was with regard to details; geographical details can be checked today against the actual terrain of Sicily and other places. In any event the sea fight described was a minor one by comparison with engagements involving over 100 ships. But regardless of whether the fight did occur at that place and time, and regardless of whether the names were actually from the Punic War period, it may be affirmed, at the very least, that the careful Silius, even if drawing upon his imagination, would have used typical names from his own or an earlier time.

Every one of the thirteen names cited from *Punica*, with the exception of *Io*, may be found in *BWN* or *MVUS68*, fifty-seven entries in all. Additionally, *Lloyd's Register of Shipping 1970–71* and *Jane's Fighting Ships 1970* together list eight of the thirteen names for ships in such countries as Argentina, Germany, Greece, Italy, Norway, and Panama. The inference appears to be that the names, or most of them, when first applied in modern times, came from *Punica* as the result of classical studies.

Whatever may be the historical truth of the *Punica* names, there can be no question about the historicity of *Isis*, the great Roman grain ship seen in the harbor at Piraeus by Lucian, the second century A.D. sophist, as described in *Navigium*.[3] This ship was about 180 feet long with 45-foot beam, a size not recorded again for commercial vessels until the sixteenth century. *Isis* was just one of Rome's large fleet of similar ships. "How gently the poop curves up, with a little golden goose below!" Lucian wrote. "And corresponding at the opposite end, the prow juts right out in front, with figures of the goddess Isis, after whom the ship is named, on either side." After describing other decorations and features of *Isis*, Lucian added, "All very wonderful to me."

About that time or somewhat earlier a Roman artist produced a tomb painting of another and smaller *Isis*, the harbor craft *Isis Giminiana*, which carried up the Tiber grain brought from Egypt by such ships as the one that thrilled Lucian. On the tomb picture, now in the Vatican Museum, the name appears (but not on the ship proper) together with the names of both captain and owner.[4]

Isis, the Egyptian goddess, was also popular among the Romans, who saw her as the prototype of the loyal wife (of Osiris) and loving mother (of Horus). I frequent a marina sheltering two sloops named *Isis*, one with a Horus figurehead. *Lloyd's* lists a Dutch freighter *Isis*; *MVUS68*, two yachts and one passenger vessel; and *BWN*, eight Royal Navy vessels of that name since 1743.

About a century earlier than Lucian's *Isis*, another grain ship with the apostle Paul aboard was wrecked at Malta, and yet another the following spring carried him on to Rome. In *Acts of the Apostles* 28 the Alexandrian ship he boarded at Malta is called *Dioscuri* (*The Twins*, Castor and Pollux). Despite arguments to the contrary, there can be little doubt —unless it is believed Luke would want to spread a pagan superstition— that by "the sign of the Twins" or "Twins on her figurehead" he meant the specific name; not some symbol intended only to invoke the patrons of seamen nor some badge indicating that Saint Elmo's fire had been seen flaring from the spars as a manifestation of the Twins. Why was the wrecked ship not also named, or the one that carried Paul's party on the first leg from Caesarea to Myra? One can only say that landlubbers are often unconcerned about such details. It is possible that *Dioscuri* seemed important to Luke because the authorities deemed it so, because it was the ship that actually delivered Paul, a prisoner, and Luke, a noncitizen, to the center of the empire. Immigration officials record such ship information today and perhaps did at that time. *Lloyd's* listed fifteen ships named *Castor* and fourteen named *Pollux* but none with both names.

From this same period the names of two Roman galleys seem to be indicated by numismatic inscriptions: *Sebastophores* (*Augustus Carrier*, or Royal Barge), which may have taken Nero to Alexandria, and *Pacatrix* (*Lady Peacemaker*), believed to have been the galley of the third-century emperor Carausius.[5]

Even if there is doubt about the names of these royal galleys, as well as the names in *Punica* and that of Saint Paul's ship, firm epigraphical evidence does exist for over eighty Roman ship names dating from the first century B.C. to several centuries after, covering the great period of imperial Rome. These ship names come from inscriptions on reliefs and columns and from other sources relating to the Roman fleets based at Misenum in southern Italy and at Ravenna on the Adriatic. These fleets in addition to the usual naval duties were active in extirpating Mediterranean pirates. Perhaps some of the ships named were merchantmen but most were certainly warships, many relatively light craft suitable for convoy and pursuit. Under "Seewesen" in Pauly-Wissowa-Kroll *Realencyclopadie der klassischen Altertumswissenschaft* are the ship names as taken from *Corpus inscriptionum Latinarum,* where the original inscriptions are reproduced.

One of these inscription names is known from another source because the dry sands of Egypt preserved a papyrus letter written during the second century A.D. by a young Egyptian recruited into Rome's navy. Addressing his father, the young man gave his newly adopted Roman name and his address: "My name is Antonius Maximus, my company Athenonica." As was customary, the company name was the same as the ship name, *Athenonica.*[6]

Examination of the complete list of names disclosed two found also in *Punica—Ammon* and *Nereis* (though *Ammon* was Carthaginian in the poem)—and also an *Isis,* after the goddess very popular with seamen.

About forty are the names of deities, although some should perhaps be termed personifications. Augustus Caesar, believing that Rome could not survive the steady erosion of religious values, revived old rites and also popularized new deities including himself. Above all, he and some of his successors sought to promote religious fervor among the military forces in order to bind them to the throne. Naming ships and ship companies after Roman gods was doubtless part of this program. Thus, the Roman trinity, consisting of the king and queen of heaven and the goddess of wisdom, was honored by *Jupiter, Juno,* and *Minerva.* There was *Apollo* for the emperor's supposed ancestor. The appeal to fighting men of the god of war was reflected in one ship called *Mars.* There were also names of new deities calculated to appeal to the population in general: *Annona* (abundant agricultural produce), *Justitia* (justice), and *Mercurius* (commercial profit). Augustus erected altars to Peace and to Fortune, and the names appeared on the ships *Pax* and *Fortuna.*

Also among the deity names—the distinction between the divine and the human sometimes being blurred—were: *Aesculapius* (healing), *Castor, Pollux, Ceres* (agriculture), *Concordia* (concord), *Danae* (mother of Perseus), *Diana* (moon), *Diomedes* (Homeric hero), *Fides* (honor), *Galeata* (perhaps the helmeted Minerva), *Hercules* (hero of heroes), *Libera* (Proserpine), *Liber pater* (Bacchus), *Libertas* (self-government of cities under ancient constitutions), *Maia* (spring), *Neptunus* (ruler of sea), *Oceanus* (waters around and under the earth), *Ops* (plenty, fertility), *Perseus* (Argive hero), *Salus* (health), *Sol* (sun), *Spes* (hope), *Sylvanus* (field and forest), *Triptolemus* (inventor of the plow), *Venus* (love), *Vesta* (hearth), *Victoria* (victory), and *Virtus* (manly valor).

Geographical names included: the rivers *Danuvius* (Danube), *Euphrates, Nilus* (Nile), *Padus* (Po), *Phryx, Rhenus* (Rhine), *Tiberis* (Tiber), and *Tigris;* the Asian mountain chain *Taurus* and the same mountains reddened by the setting sun *Taurus ruber*; and *Armenia* and names deriving from Dacia and Parthia, *Daciens* and *Parthicus*.

Among others were *Aquila* for the eagle, *Capricornus* for the zodiac goat, *Cupido* (desire), *Felix* (happy), *Juventus* (youth), *Lucifer* (the planet Venus as a morning star), *Murena* (a lamprey or a Roman family), *Pietas* (duty to country or respect for the gods), and *Radians* (gleaming as referring to the moon). *Salamina* recalled Salamis and like *Athenonica* was one of several Greek echoes. The aforementioned *Cupido* might have referred to a religious spring ceremony in which associations of small children (cupids) drew large ship models in procession at the opening of the new navigation season.[7]

The ship name *Salvia* obviously derives from the ship supposed to have transported from Pergamum in Asia to Rome the sacred black stone of the Great Mother of the gods, Cybele, about 191 B.C. According to legend, *Salvia* stuck on a sandbar at the entrance to the Tiber and could not be freed until a vestal virgin fastened her girdle to the prow and drew the ship up river to the Palatine, where a temple had been prepared for the stone.[8]

A comparison of these Roman names with the examples from Greece shows a sharp difference in spirit between the two peoples, or at least between their rulers. That several centuries intervened and that the Roman deity names reflected political calculations do not alone account for this difference. A fundamentally different outlook upon life is also apparent in art, architecture, and government, the Greek attitude containing much that was light and lyrical, even on occasion superficial, as against the Roman heavy, matter-of-fact determination. Although a number of the names are identical, such as *Liberty, Peace, Youth, Morning Star (Lucifer)*, and *Victory*, the Greek examples generally lack the Roman personifications of duty, patriotism, commerce, and solid virtues. Roman nomenclature included all the known world's rivers, where Roman ships carried on trade or flotillas pursued pirates. It must be remembered, however, that most Roman names were also designations for the assigned naval companies, and consequently Greek names that might suggest fine handling qualities in a galley or the beauty of a woman were not suitable for a military unit. Still, if such Greek names as *Charming* or *Beloved* were ruled out, names such as *Audacious* or *Excellent* would seem apt, although they probably never occurred to the grave officials of Rome.

CHAPTER IV

Medieval Ships

14. Medieval Europe

I N THE medieval period ship names probably differed little from those already examined except for the substitution of Christian names for some pagan names. While some nautical historians claim that during the early medieval period ships lacked names, there is no reason to suppose Roman custom did not survive the breakup of the empire, simply because recorded names are lacking until almost A.D. 1200.[1] Probably the tendency was strong to identify commercial ships for trade purposes by the owner's name—that is, by the name of the *nauclerus*, or manager, who might be full or part owner or merely a nominee. Under Rhodian and other early sea law this individual had power to collect and disburse money, to borrow on the credit of the ship, and even to sell the ship.

Names of a few early English ships have been preserved. There was *Countess*, apparently a prize, given by King John in 1212 to William, earl of Salisbury.[2] Seemingly, the earl protested she was old and useless, for another was substituted. *Queen* was a king's ship in the reign of Henry III (1216–1272), chartered by one John Blancbully for his lifetime at an annual cost of fifty marks on condition he would return the ship on demand in event of war.[3] In 1227 the "great ship" *Cardinal* headed a force under Richard de Grey to take Guernsey and Jersey.[4] Note that all three of these English ships had generic title names. Even earlier, *White Ship* (about 1120), although apparently not English, was much used by Henry I and Henry II as a channel ferry for troops and could carry 300 men. It is thought that *Christopher of the Tower*, so named because employed by the crown, was the first English ship to have a gun put aboard, in 1406.[5]

The Venetians were prominent as ship builders and charterers over a long period. The largest ship they provided Saint Louis in 1268 was *Holy Mary* (*Sancta Maria*), length 108 feet, beam 70 feet, a veritible dish, and another they supplied him was *Saint Nicholas*.[6] Another dish-shaped craft offered Saint Louis was called *Roccaforte*, which carried twenty anchors and could transport 500 soldiers.[7]

The Genoese were active, too, in supplying ships for crusaders and pilgrims. Saint Louis hired *San Salvador* from them, a two-mast ship

handled by twenty-two men and three boys.[8] *Olivia* and *Great Paradise*
(*Paradisus magnus*) on the run between Genoa and Syria were typical
passenger or cargo ships of about 1250. *Olivia* carried 1,100 pilgrims with
a crew of 75; *Great Paradise* with a crew of 100 was rated for 600 tons of
cargo.[9] Mentioned in Villehardouin's chronicle of the Fourth Crusade
was an earlier *Paradise*, perhaps from Genoa, which was prominent in
the assault on Constantinople in 1204. *Paradise* was lashed to another
ship called *Pilgrim*, and the ladder platform thus formed sailed beneath
a tower, which was successfully taken.[10]

Among French ships from this period, *Saint Francis*, a buss of about
1248, carried 300 pilgrims, while *Saint Leonard*, of the same type and
period, had space for 200.[11] Also mentioned in old contracts between
owners and charterers were *Boreata*, a galley built at Marseilles in 1248,
carrying freight between its two decks; *Saint Vincent* from Marseilles;
and *Saint Nicholas*, 240 tons with crew of 118, part of a fleet collected in
1340 for war with England.[12]

The Venetians continued to supply ships for some centuries. Their
ships and many others fought at Lepanto in 1571. The prior of the Order
of Saint John commanded the Maltese flagship *Capitana*, which means
"captain's ship" but is an actual name none the less. *San Giovanni* and
Piamontesea were among the ships from Savoy. *Florence* and *Maiden*
(*Doncella*) were mentioned among the combatants. Cervantes was
wounded aboard *Marquesa*, one of Andrea Doria's galleys.[13] In discuss-
ing the campaign of Lepanto, Vice Admiral W. L. Rodgers observed that
apart from her given name a ship was often known by the feminine form
of her captain's surname. Thus *Brigandina* referred to either of the
two galleasses commanded by the brothers Ambrosio and Antonio
Brigandino.[14]

Linking owners to ships is not unusual, being one of the earliest means
of ship identification. Apparently the tendency is strong for the community, whether a small fishing village or a large commercial region, to think
of a ship in terms of the owner. Records and diaries confirm this fact, as
illustrated by an old and typical official Venetian entry: "Item, nave de
sier Piero Ruzeir." Often the ship and owner do bear the same name, such
as *Blasius Alberegno* (1426) and *Giovanni Contareno* (1430) for Venetian ships.[15] On a broader geographical and chronological scale, ships
known for a person frequently have had a different official name. The
ships of Columbus offer good examples. His favorite *Niña* was officially
Santa Clara, after the patron saint of Mogeus, but she belonged to her
master, Juan Niño of Palos. *Pinta* was supposedly named after a previous
owner, a member of the Pinto family, and her official name is now un-

known. The third of the original Columbian trio, *Santa Maria*, was known to those aboard as *Galician* (*Gallega*), perhaps because she or her owner came from there, perhaps because she was slow and heavy-working and thus some reference to the Galician character was intended. *Santiago de Palos*, a caravel of the fourth Columbus voyage, was known as *Bermuda* after her master, Francisco Bermúdez.[16]

15. Viking Warships

For the period from about 1600 onward, only occasional reference will be made to ship naming outside the English-speaking world. However, mention should be made, though somewhat late as regards chronology, of Viking names, which constitute a type rather different from those of cultures deriving more directly from the Graeco-Roman world. As was true of Grecian and Roman names, the Viking names were almost entirely those of warcraft. Perpetuated principally in the Norse sagas, these names were for longships in the period of naval warfare from about 1000 to 1300.

Some Viking names have been poetized in translation into such compounds as *Snake of the Sea* and *Deer of the Surf*, which resemble the poetic names of such American clipper ships as *Herald of the Morning* (1853) and *Champion of the Seas* (1854). However, the meaning may be closer to the original if the translation is taken from the English version of *The Viking Ships*, largely the work of Dr. A. W. Brögger, from which, unless otherwise noted, all information on Viking names will be taken.[1] Unfortunately, the names of ordinary Norse ships used for trade and transport and exploration have not survived, but very likely they were similar to longship names, though perhaps less grandiose and warlike.

In ship naming did the Vikings adopt a practice observed in use by other peoples? They had contact by sea with the rest of Europe and via Russia's rivers with Byzantium; Sigurd the Crusader even took a fleet to the Aegean in the early twelfth century. Or did Viking ship names develop slowly? We only know that by the year 995 names were in use, for in that year Norway's king, Olav Tryggvason, launched *Crane*, with sixty oars and from 140 to 164 feet overall. According to Brögger, the name probably derived from the stem rising (like the stern) high in the air to suggest the neck of a crane. The King thought his longboat was the largest and finest anywhere until he sailed to Salten to visit a rich freeholder, Raud the Strong, whose splendid sixty-oar *Short Serpent* excited his envy and led to Raud's downfall. About a year later the king launched Norway's most famous ship, *Long Serpent* (1000), having sixty-eight oars; it probably was not exceeded in size for about 200 years. The boat taken from Raud, perhaps originally known as *Serpent*, later became *Short Serpent* to distinguish it from *Long Serpent*.

A characteristic of Viking names is the predilection for references to serpents, both land and sea types. In fact, the ships were often termed "dragons" or "sea serpents." Vikings of great strength were called *orms*, possibly referring to the type of creature thought to survive in Loch Ness today. *Encyclopaedia Britannica* cites "Serpent of the Wound" as a sword name, like "Viper of the Host," and mentions both "Snake of the Attack" and "Shooting Serpent" as spears. Brögger observed that the serpent, which in ancient magic was both a guardian power and a threat to enemies, became an enduring symbol in the Norse folk psyche and even carried over into Christian times. The unearthing of the burial ship at Oseberg showed that ancient despoilers, before plundering the burial chamber, took the precaution of cutting up the serpent prow ornament placed with the royal corpse as a guard. In the Christian period the serpent or sea serpent appeared on architectural decorations and jewelry and even on a bishop's crozier. Many Viking ships carried removable serpent or dragon heads, surmounting the sweeping curve of the prow, and curling tails at the stern; these decorations persisted into the Christian period. A law from pagan times required the removal of these guardian heads before the ship made land, in order not to frighten the good homeland spirits.

Viking ships, Brögger speculated, at first were named for the prow ornament. About 1016 the saintly Olav II had a longship called *The Man's Head* after the prow figure said to have been carved by the saint himself, perhaps in an attempt to minimize the serpent superstition. In 1026 Saint Olav had the sixty-oar *Bison* with an ox head on the prow. *Serpent, Dragon,* and *Ox* as names for smaller ships may have originated in this way.

From about 1150 onward, in Brögger's view, the names reflected Christianity and kingship in evolution. King Erling Wryneck, leader of the church party, launched *Saint Olav's Ship* (1170) as part of his appeal to national history in seeking to impose Christian order and direction. In 1182 King Sverre christened *Mary's Ship* and in his dedication gave thanks for the successful launching, put the ship under the protection of the Virgin Mary, announced his gift of rich church vestments in her honor, and concluded: "I expect that she will remember all these gifts and give aid and luck both to the ship and all who fare in it."

From *Mary's Ship* to the last-mentioned longship of sixty oars or more, which was the seventy-four oar *Christ's Ship* (1263) launched by King Haakon, only one longship—*Menacing Ship* (1199)—had a nonreligious name. In the interim there were another *Saint Olav's Ship* of uncertain date, a *Good Friday* (1233), a *Holy Cross* (1252), and another *Mary's Ship* (1257). *Christ's Ship* was the largest Norse ship of the Middle Ages and was built as the royal flagship for the Scottish expedition of King Magnus III. It brought his body home from the Orkney Islands.

The Vikings also had many standard warships of forty to fifty oars, but these did not impress the bards, and few names have survived. Some surviving names originated in Christianity; others were nonreligious. One rather curious name was *Hrefa* (1181), designating the fifth plank in the strakes of a forty-oar ship. *Beard* (1181) had a bearded male head at the prow. *Reindeer* was used several times. Three names date from the year 1184, *Help*, *Valkyrie*, and *Ship One Must Beware Of*. A bishop had a ship called *Redside*, presumably painted red and not intended for war. One famous ship, taken from its original owner by King Sverre and last mentioned when not less than fifty-six years old as belonging to King Hakkon, very likely had a gilded prow suggesting its name *Goldenbreast*. English custom records of 1304 listed *Heartease* and *Ox* from Norway. Over two centuries earlier William the Conqueror crossed to England in *Mora*, a Viking-type ship, manned by warriors probably descended from Norsemen who settled in Normandy.

CHAPTER V

Markings—Ancient and Modern

16. Written Names and Other Markings

IT PROBABLY will never be known for certain when written names first appeared on ships. As mentioned earlier, Petrie supposed that simple names of certain Egyptian stone-carrying boats might have been shown on the bow by single-sign hieroglyphs. *Greek Oared Ships* pictures an ivory plaque of 650 to 600 B.C. from Sparta's Temple of Artemis Orthia showing a ship with the word *Orthaia* [*sic*] on the bow, which R. T. Williams suggested might have been the name of the ship as well as of the goddess to which the plaque was dedicated.[1] Alexander McKee in *History under the Sea* discussed the Pantano Longarini wreck found in 1963 in a marsh of southeastern Sicily.[2] This forty-meter craft was carbon dated to about A.D. 500. The men who found the ship, after having destroyed some fifteen meters of planking on the upper starboard side, later told the archaeologists that this woodwork had included a hardwood plaque affixed to the stem post and inscribed with a horse's head and five or six Greek letters. This inscription, in McKee's opinion, clearly was the name of the ship. If McKee was incorrect in this assumption, it appears no firm evidence for written names on ships dates from earlier than the sixteenth century, despite the probability that the practice has a remote history. It cannot be assumed that there were no historical gaps in the use of written names.

Early ships of some lands in some periods doubtless were identified by emblems, either representing the names exactly or suggesting names that were complex or abstract. Such emblems would make recognition possible, particularly for the unlettered, even if a written name were also used. Similarly, some ship figureheads of recent times represented names, whereas others had little or no connection with them. Figureheads were primarily for ornamentation, as were the paddlebox artistry on sidewheel steamers, the elaborate decorations at the stern of seventeenth-century sailing ships, and the prow badges on some modern merchant vessels. Certainly, the same human motives prompted the ancients to decorate their ships. Yet some emblems and decorations must have served an additional purpose. In the Greek and Phoenician worlds removable stern ornaments and devices painted on the hull indicated nationality and perhaps squadrons within national fleets. A captured enemy stern ornament was a sign of triumph. At sea, especially in the thick of battle, hull markings or banners would be more quickly identified than names.

Not that an experienced sailor, once having studied a particular ship, would need a name for identification; for the sailor's practiced eye readily detects small differences among apparently identical craft. But the merchant, the agent, and the officers of the temple and the palace required some positive means of identification, and there is no reason to suppose they could all read. However, anybody could identify by symbol. When King Richard II sailed to Ireland in 1399 on a ship believed to have been *Sun in Splendour*, a sun symbol appeared on the mainsail, and not improbably that symbol appeared prominently on the hull.[3]

A further possibility is that it may no more have occurred to some early peoples to paint a name on a ship than to paint one on the forehead of a person, absurd as this may seem. Thus, in some places, a ship's name could have been learned as a person's name was learned—by being told.

Another minor consideration is that of secrecy. Secret names among not-so-primitive people have already been mentioned; the name was considered part of the essential person or thing, and knowledge of it could mean power gained by an enemy in the material or the spiritual world.

Artists, both ancient and medieval, like most artists today, either did not consider it important to show written ship names or used media that would not permit such fine detail. Thus no pictorial evidence exists of when or how ship names were first applied. Ignoring the previously mentioned temple plaque of *Orthaia*, because it cannot be assumed that the name appeared on the bow of the actual ship, there is a gap of about 4,000 years between the first known names and the first positively known written names on ships.

Because of the ritual importance of the bow, it might be inferred that written names first appeared there, although a good case can be made for the stern, where names first appear pictorially, for the shrine to a god or goddess on many ancient ships of the Mediterranean world was located at the stern. However, since a name has commercial value for a merchant ship, its location in different times and places may have varied, as it has in recent centuries. Name location could depend upon whether a ship was loaded over the side, over the bow, or over the stern, since easy visibility from the loading area would be important. Also, the design details of a particular vessel could dictate name positioning, as could the way it was stored in a shipyard when drawn from the water. All things considered, we can only speculate.

Nautical archaeologists are not likely to be of much help. Timbers from really old wrecks are usually decayed, with any paint gone. Names could at times have been carried on some superficial standard. The possibility does exist of finding a carved name, such as that supposed to have been on the previously mentioned seventh-century wreck unearthed in Sicily. Carved names were not found on the elaborately carved Oseberg burial ship or on other Viking-period ships uncovered from mounds.

It is almost axiomatic that crafts and customs actually have much earlier origins than reliable evidence suggests. Thus, without knowing whether the practice was new or old, it can be said that by the sixteenth century some European ships had written names at the stern, and that by the late eighteenth century the practice was common.

A picture of a Dutch ship by Bruegel, according to an anonymous contributor of a note in *The Mariner's Mirror*, has "Die ———, 1564" across the stern, the actual name being illegible.[4] Two old paintings reproduced in *5000 Jahre Segelschiffe* show stern names with dates.[5] The oldest painting is of *Eagle* (*Der Adler*, 1566) of Lübeck, a six-decked warship about 200 feet in length, begun during a war with Sweden but not completed and later cut down into a merchantman. The other contemporary painting shows *Amilia* (1634), flagship of Admiral Marten Trump. Another book of marine paintings reproduces one showing *Prince William* (*Prins Willem*, 1651) with her name and date and the initials of the United East India Company on the stern.[6] Onward from the middle of the seventeenth century, stern names, sometimes almost lost among the elaborate galleries and carved decorations, appear in numerous paintings.

Apparently English ships were not required (unless by local custom) to show name and registry port until 1786, although certainly ship name and port had been associated long before, even earlier than in the examples *John of Greenwich* (1523) and *Jesus of Lubeck* (1544).[7] In 1660 under Charles II the first national register of ships was established to ascertain which ships were to benefit from the Navigation Act of 1651. That act required owners and masters of ships flying the national flag to be British subjects but was silent about markings. In 1696 an act during the reign of William and Mary dealt with ship registration but made no mention of painting the name of ship or port. Apparently it was "An Act for the Increase and Encouragement of Shipping," passed in 1786, that first made obligatory the painting of names of ship and port on the sterns of English merchantmen. This act in section 19 stated that many frauds were committed by frequent changes of name, and therefore it specified:

That it shall not be lawful for any owner or owners of any ship or vessel to give any name to such ship or vessel, other than that by which she was first registered in pursuance of this act; and that the owner or owners of all and every ship or vessel which shall be so registered, shall, within one month from the time of such registry, paint or cause to be painted, in white or yellow letters, of a length not less than four inches, upon a black ground, on some conspicuous part of the stern (provided there shall be sufficient space for that purpose, but if not then in letters as large as such space will admit) the name by which such ship or vessel shall have been registered pursuant to this act, and the port to which she belongs, in a distinct and legible manner, and shall so keep and preserve the same; and that if such owner or owners or master or other person having or taking the charge or command of such ship or vessel, shall wilfully alter, erase, obliterate, or in any way hide or conceal, or cause or procure, or permit the same to be done, unless in the case of square-rigged vessels in time of war, or shall in any written or printed paper, or other document, describe such ship or vessel by any name, other than that by which she was first registered pursuant to this act, or shall verbally describe, or cause or procure or permit such ship or vessel to be described, by any other name, to any officer or officers of his Majesty's revenue, in the due execution of his or their duty, then, and in every such case, such owner or owners, master, or other person having or taking the charge or command of such ship or vessel, shall forfeit the sum of one hundred pounds.[8]

This registry act is quoted in some detail because it preceded by about two years the first such United States law. It specifically could not be applied to ships built in the "colonies of North America, now called the United States of America," or to ships of United States citizens unless such ships were taken and judged as lawful prizes. Also excluded from the provisions of the act—including the required display of name and port—were lighters, barges, boats used solely on rivers or for inland navigation, and craft belonging to any member of the royal family.

Although English merchant ships were required by law to display painted names after 1786, the Royal Navy during the American Revolution found it disadvantageous to show such names, and soon after the Revolution, when Augustus Keppel became first lord of the Admiralty in 1782, the practice ceased. Keppel claimed that it would be better to paint the names small upon panels, presumably for easy removal to thwart enemy intelligence, following the old French and Spanish practice.[9]

Names on United States naval vessels today are in relatively small thin letters, black on gray, and are frequently only at the stern and visible for a short distance only. Sometimes small nameboards are carried on the superstructure. Identification depends upon numerals, or letters combined with numerals, painted large upon hull or superstructure, a highly visible shorthand that conveys to the initiated not only the name but also the type and build sequence within the type. In wartime hull numbers and other identification may be painted over. Significantly, the desirability—for visitors if not for others—for Navy and Coast Guard vessels to be clearly identified while at berth is evidenced by the fact that the names (sometimes with hull numbers) are painted large upon canvas stretched along the sides of gangplanks. Occasionally, also, open-topped canvas sacks, each painted with one letter of a ship's name (if the name is not too long), are hung from a horizontal line over a lifeboat or somewhere near the gangway. Stowed in these sacks for easy removal are lifelines or "monkey lines" for emergency use in descending quickly to a boat below.

The importance of clear identification to avoid confusion in war or distress is illustrated by the Confederate steamboat *William G. Hewes* (1860), which should have been renamed when taken by Union forces instead of merely having the original name shortened to *Hewes*. Thereafter she was variously entered into records as *Henes, Hawes, Heines,* and even as *Jewess*.[10] (There was, incidentally, an authentic *Jewess* (1838) built for the Chesapeake Bay and later used in coastal service until lost in 1856).[11]

Sailing ships of the nineteenth and the early twentieth century, when the wheel was located well aft, had a box over the steering mechanism abaft the wheel. This box was clearly visible over the sides and frequently had the ship's name carved and/or painted on each side. On the sidewheel steamer the paddlebox offered the obvious location for name and decorations, and even after the advent of the screw propeller the name remained large upon the hull of some ships where the paddlebox had been located. Steamboats on inland American waters frequently had a large nameboard across the front of the pilothouse as well as at each side. Today many boats for sport fishermen have the name in large letters across the front of the superstructure, where it will be clearly seen by anglers who may be comparing boats before buying tickets.

In the days of sail, names occasionally appeared on sails, as on pilot schooners, for easy identification at sea. A drawing from about 1795 shows small American schooners, obviously not all pilot craft, with names on foresails, and a Robert Salmon painting of the packet ship *United States* (1817) shows her name on the foretopsail.[12] Clipper ships in port not infrequently used a studding sail to advertise the next passage, lettered with the names of the ship, the destination, and the agent. Pilot schooners often showed their hailing port as well as the name on the sails.

Trail boards at the bows of a sailing vessel invited application of a name, and a few old photos do show such usage; but this practice was exceptional, perhaps because this location, not being on the hull proper, did not satisfy registry requirements. Sailing yachts of the twentieth century sometimes carry names on the boards supporting the sidelights, the boards frequently being attached to shrouds, where the names are dimly illuminated by the red and green running lights.

Many sailing vessels, at least from the early nineteenth century, on occasion flew pennants displaying the name (or sometimes only the initials or a portion of a long name). Old paintings and photos show such pennants usually flying from the mainmast on brigs and ships and from the aftermost mast on schooners. Customarily, a flag, usually rectangular, bearing the name, the initials, or symbols of the line, flew on a mast ahead of the name pennant. Flag etiquette varied, however, as it does today.

Most present-day merchant ships also have name flags. Unlike the house flag, which flies all the time, the name flag only appears on special occasions, such as on Christmas and other holidays, or when the ship is dressed with signal flags. The lettering on name flags is customarily black on a white background, perhaps with a border of red or other color. The name flag is sometimes a gift to the captain, sewn by his wife or female acquaintance, or is obtained from a commercial source.

The modern use of names on the bow developed gradually and was not universal even late in the nineteenth century. Actually, it was the tragic loss of 293 lives on *Norfleet* (1853) that made the painting of names on each bow obligatory for British ships. The clipper *Norfleet*, while at anchor riding out a gale in the English Channel, was cut down in 1873 by the Spanish steamer *Murillo*. Because *Murillo* had no name displayed forward, survivors could not identify her when she backed off and fled the scene. Later, she was identified in a continental port by her damaged bow.[13] Under a prompt amendment to shipping laws all British ships after January 1, 1874, were to display the name on each bow in letters at least four inches high—white or yellow letters on a dark ground or black letters on a light ground.[14]

In 1845, prior to the *Murillo* incident, the United Kingdom had passed a registration act that did not change marking requirements, but the Merchant Shipping Act of 1854 required that the tonnage and the number of the registry certificate be "deeply carved or otherwise permanently marked" on the ship's main beam.[15] A few years later a system of official numbers independent of the certificate was instituted. The 1854 act exempted from registration river and coastal vessels of less than fifteen tons burden, together with undecked or partially decked fishing or trading vessels operating in the Gulf of Saint Lawrence and in the vicinity of Newfoundland. While the act prohibited changing the name of a registered vessel, it permitted reregistration if desired (and presumably a change of name) upon any change of ownership.

Current legislation for the United Kingdom is contained in the Merchant Shipping Acts of 1894 and 1906.[16] Fishing boats still constitute a special class and need not have name and port marked if they are entered into the fishing boat register, under which they carry letters and numbers. Otherwise the ship's name must be marked on each bow, and the name and registry port at the stern. The marking must be on a dark ground in white or yellow letters or on a light ground in black letters, such letters to be not less than four inches in height and of proportionate width. The only statutory restriction with regard to names authorizes the Board of Trade (now the Department of Trade and Industry) to refuse registry if another British ship bears the same name or a name so similar as to be calculated to deceive.

A letter to me in December of 1971 from the General Register and Record Office of Shipping and Seamen states: "Although we make every endeavour to avoid duplication of names, we do in certain circumstances permit this provided the vessels concerned are not of similar size or type. There is no restriction on the length of a name, and we have agreed, on request, to the use of foreign characteres (e.g. Greek or Chinese) provided that the name is also shown in English." The letter goes on to say that, while not required, the submission of alternate names on application often saves time, and that unsuitable names (including *Mayday* and names of certain members of the royal family) are rejected.

The Act of 1894 sets forth the procedure for changing a name. "In practice," the aforementioned letter states, "applicants must obtain the approval of this office to any name which it is proposed to use and must advertise their intention of changing the name in two newspapers circulating in the port of registry to give any interested parties an opportunity to object if they so wish."

British law requires that a vessel's official number and registered tonnage be cut into the main beam, prohibits the use of any nickname or unofficial name, and states that the only acceptable excuse for concealing or altering a ship's markings is for purposes of escaping capture by an enemy.

Because the United States has a heritage of English customs and common law, regulations regarding ship names and registry in general follow those of Great Britain. Perhaps the most obvious difference is that unlimited duplication of names is permitted in the United States. Precise identification depends upon the six-digit number assigned at the time of documentation. This number remains with the ship as long as she exists and is never reassigned. On a wooden vessel the number must be carved on the main beam in figures not less than three-eighths inch in depth; on a metal vessel, be outlined on the main beam by center punching; and on a fiberglass vessel, be shown clearly on a plate bonded permanently inside the hull. The net tonnage of the ship must be shown in the same manner. All figures must be painted over in a light color on a dark ground. The main beam is defined as that at the forward end of the largest hatch on the weather deck. If no main beam as such exists, the figures are put on a suitable structural member integral with the hull.

Prior to the Declaration of Independence in 1776, ships of the American colonies were supposed to follow British marking practice. During the interim years of the Continental Congress, ship owners doubtless continued the same practice. Then with the beginning of constitutional government in the spring of 1789 the need for navigation laws became apparent. It should be kept in mind that registration laws for ships differ in purpose from those for pleasure craft and automobiles. The registered merchant ship benefits greatly by conditions of trade denied foreign ships, and always it enjoys the protection of its nation's flag. The nation is less concerned with controlling smugglers or providing a means for recording debts against documented vessels than it is with fostering international trade and excluding foreign ships from coastal trade, as well as encouraging shipbuilding, often by subsidies, so that bottoms will be available in national emergency.

Thus, among the earliest acts passed during the first session of the United States Congress was that of September 1, 1789, entitled "An Act for the Registry and Clearing of Vessels, Regulating the Coastal Trade, and for Other Purposes."[17] With respect to markings, this act specified that the name of a registered vessel and the port to which she belonged should "be painted on her stern, on a black ground with white letters of not less than three inches in length." The first registration of a vessel was to be under her existing name. Any subsequent name change was to be accomplished by the owner or agent by having a memorandum endorsed on the certificate of registry, by the Collector of the district where such ship might be or where she arrived from a foreign country with a new name. In order to be classed as a United States vessel, those of twenty tons or more employed in the coasting trade or fisheries were to be enrolled and to show their name and port on the stern in the manner of a registered vessel.

Two years later the act of December 31, 1792, required the same markings as the previous law but specified a forfeit of $50, one half to go to the informant, for each failure to display the name properly at all times.

Three quarters of a century elapsed before the next change involving ship markings. During the Civil War the small lettering at the stern was found to be insufficient for easy identification. The war tempted some ship owners into illegal activities; the navy was spread thin; surveillance on inland rivers was often by the army from shore batteries. Therefore, "An Act for the Prevention and Punishment of Frauds in Relation to the Names of Vessels" was adopted May 5, 1864, and specified that steamships should, in addition to the usual markings at the stern, have the name in plain letters not less than six inches high on each side of the pilothouse and also on the outer side of each wheelhouse if the vessel had sidewheels. The act likewise provided for the forfeiture of the vessel if any owner, master, or agent in any way changed the name of the vessel, actually or by advertisement, or attempted to deceive authorities or the public as to the true name.

An act of July 28, 1866, authorized the secretary of the treasury to establish a numbering system, each vessel to have the number deeply carved or otherwise permanently marked on her main beam. These numbers were first assigned by reserving blocks for vessels with names beginning with the same letter and by separating rigged from unrigged ships. Thus the initial *A* got the block 1–1,999 (rigged) and 29,000–30,999 (unrigged); *B* got 2,000–3,999 and 31,000–32,999, and so on. If the first blocks ran out, low numbers in the six-digit series were assigned. Finally, on July 1, 1903, unrigged vessels with names starting from *A* to *Z* got the block 162,000–199,999, and rigged vessels with the same initial letters got 200,000 plus.

Several years later the act of June 23, 1874, permitted names marked in yellow or gilt letters. This was in a period of gold-leaf decorations on steamboats, especially those competing on the Mississippi and other inland waters.

As could be expected, for reasons mentioned in the section "Name Changes," many shipowners objected to the 1864 prohibition against name changing (a prohibition that was repeated in the act of February 28, 1871, along with the identical steamboat marking requirements). These objections probably explain the passage of special congressional acts to accomplish what the registry laws forbade. For example, acts dated June 14, 1880, changed the name of the sloop *Mariah* of Rochester to *Tourist* and that of *E. R. Bryant* of Rochester to *Summerland*. On March 2, 1881, authority to change names of seaworthy vessels free from debt was vested in the secretary of the treasury, contingent upon publication of such changes in at least four issues of a newspaper at the place of register. This requirement is still in force today, except that ship documentation now comes under the Department of Transportation, United States Coast Guard.

Revisions to the navigation statutes as of February 21, 1891, and January 20, 1897, generally are in force today as regards markings, with minor revisions in 1920, 1932, and 1936 and perhaps in other years. Pertinent statutes today include Revised Statute 4177 (46 United States Code 45), RS 4178 (46 USC 46), RS 4179 (46 USC 50, 51, 52), and RS 4495 (46 USC 493).[18]

Although in 1891 vessels for the first time were required to show the name on each bow, this proviso was interpreted as not mandatory for vessels already under registry, because the amending act of 1897 granted vessels already registered the remainder of that year in which to comply. Originally, the lettering on the bow was to be a minimum of six inches high; presently the minimum is four inches high. Every steamship is still required to have her name in minimum six-inch letters on each outer side of the pilothouse. On vessels with square bows, the name may be marked across the front rather than on both sides. On double-enders the stern name and port designation may be marked on adjacent parts as near as possible to the after end.

Name and port are to be painted or gilded, in cut or carved or cast roman letters, in light color on a dark ground or vice versa, permanently secured in place, and distinctly visible. The home port is defined as the place where the vessel is enrolled or registered, or the place in the same district where built, or the place where an owner resides.

Forfeiture of the vessel is still the possible penalty for illegal change or concealment of the true name.

Responsibility for ship documentation was transferred as of February 24, 1967, from the United States Customs to the United States Coast Guard. The actual awarding of the number and signal letters and the approval of the name are by the chief, Merchant Vessel Documentation Division, U.S.C.G., Department of Transportation. No specific rules limit choice of name, but names considered unsuitable are not approved. Documentation is often done through a customhouse broker familiar with the procedure, since some transactions require the submission of no less than seven forms, certificates, or affidavits, some in duplicate or triplicate, from owners, builders, mortgagee, and others. Applications are filed with the documentation officer at principal ports.

Many large vessels of other countries, besides having the usual name at bows and stern, tend to follow the American usage of having the name also at each side of the pilothouse, usually on boards but sometimes painted directly on the structure. Also a few show the name and home port on each side at the stern (even though they are not double-ended) and may dispense with pilothouse names.

Flags of convenience, particularly those of Liberia and Panama, fly from many vessels. Over 2,000 foreign ships display Liberian colors, of which about 500 are American owned, while Panama has over 1,000 foreign documentations. Advantages involving taxes, unions, and safety regulations are among the varied reasons for documentation under foreign flags. The right to display the Liberian flag is granted any foreign, seagoing, trading vessel of 1,600 tons or more that is less than twenty years old when documented. An official number is assigned. Requirements for displaying the name and port are the same as those for the United States, practically word for word. However, duplication of names for active vessels is not permitted. The procedure for name changing is similar to that of the United States and the United Kingdom. Panama, likewise, generally follows United States marking requirements but like Liberia does not permit duplication of names.

On many vessels the nameboards on the pilothouse are of mahogany with gold letters, a survival from olden days on ships otherwise of steel. A few proud captains illuminate the names on the house at night by using searchlights at the wings of the bridge. Some owners provide illuminated signs, customarily larger than the usual nameboards. These signs are usually limited to ships that carry some passengers or only passengers. The signs may be of the neon type or on glass illuminated from behind with dark letters on a translucent background or translucent letters on a dark background. The luxury liner *France* (1962) advertised herself in port by showing her name in lights in separate man-size letters, facing port and starboard on the top deck between funnels. A few Asian vessels have lighted signs in Asiatic characters and in English on the pilothouse.

Since language can be a barrier in trade, ship names are often translated or transliterated. Asian ships trading with English-speaking countries usually show name and hailing port both in characters and in letters on bows and stern. Greek ships usually have the name in Latin letters on the bows, while Russian freighters show the name in Latin letters only on pilothouse boards, generally using a Polish or German orthography. Ships both from and trading among countries using the Latin alphabet do not have names translated; in fact, to do so would cause endless confusion.

Möller Line freighters—all having names including the surname "Maersk"—are the only vessels I have seen that carried the name in man-size letters on each side of the hull amidships in the position where many ships show line designations. As vessels grow larger, however, there appears to be a trend toward showing correspondingly larger, even occasionally up to man-size, lettering on the bows, as in the case of *Dilkara*, London, a roll-on-and-off freighter. In wartime, to make identification easier for submarines, neutral ships may use oversize markings and sometimes shine lights on the names at night. During World War I Germany attempted to require neutrals in the war zone to show illuminated identification or be sunk. This demand was rejected by the United States before she entered the war. In World War II steamers often removed nameboards from pilothouses and had names painted out on bows and stern.

Merchant ships customarily have their stacks painted distinctively to identify the line. In at least one instance the stack color provided the shipping firm's name, the Blue Funnel Line. Stacks often carry horizontal bands of color and/or show symbols or reproduce the house flag. Only in rare instances do such symbols indicate a name; for example, some small vessel might show a daisy on the stack for *Daisy*.

The bow badge, a survival of the figurehead, is another means of identification on many modern vessels. Occasionally this badge, high on the prow, indicates the name; for example, a figure hurling thunderbolts would represent *Thor*. A badge may portray the old Hanseatic seal or other symbol of the vessel's home port, such as the three-towered castle for Hamburg. In most cases, however, the badge indicates the line and often duplicates the house flag.

Ship color as a whole may also identify the ship or the line; for instance, light blue hulls identify Möller ships, and pumpkin orange topsides and light green superstructure, Barber Line vessels. The color scheme for most lines, however, typically consists of black or, less frequently, white topsides, with the superstructure a light contrasting color, usually white or tan. Masts and cargo-handling equipment may be the same color as the superstructure but may show a third color, frequently tan. Shades of blue, green, gray, tan, and red on the topsides introduce variety in any large harbor.

To facilitate the repainting by unskilled sailors of the names and hailing port, weld-beading may be used to define the edges of the markings, or raised letters may be cut out of metal and welded in place. Thus when names are changed, the evidence of previous names cannot always be removed completely and may be seen beneath new paint.

The need for ship identification from the air affects ship markings. United States aircraft carriers have long shown their numbers painted large upon the flight decks, and British carriers, the first letter of the

name. Some offshore oil-drilling and other specialized vessels with regular commutation by helicopter have markings visible from above. Aerial
fish spotters, however, who cooperate by radio with a limited number of
known vessels in locating schools of fish and in directing netting operations, appear to have no need for special markings. In search-and-rescue
operations it would be helpful if small craft had names clearly visible
from the air. To make icebreakers more visible against the Arctic white
for helicopters and other aircraft, the United States Coast Guard painted
over in bright red the traditional white topsides of some vessels.

Modern Ships—Name Sources

17. Name Popularity

WITH few exceptions, the ship names mentioned so far have been those of warships or state-owned vessels, because these were important enough to have been entered into the records. However, ships engaged in trade, fishing, and other maritime activity always far outnumber warships, and from about 1500 onward the importance of commercial vessels is increasingly reflected in the records.

In the following sections ship names will be categorized by types, with suitable illustrations from different periods, to show the development, the continuity, and the changes in ship nomenclature, as well as to indicate current practices. Among the classifications will be the following: feminine, masculine, geographical, paired, generic, titled, mythological, religious, political, numerical, functional, heroic, and unusual. Other aspects of ship naming covered will be: names in series, names changed, names reflecting contemporary influences, names favored by explorers, and names as parts of speech.

That time affects the choice of names is evident in names already mentioned, as well as those to follow. Although certain type names persist through the millenniums—that is, *person* names, *place* names, *thing* names, *abstract* names—the popularity of a type and its subdivisions changes with alterations in outlook brought about by location, nationality, war, politics, economics, ship size, ship use, and just plain fad or fancy. One type ship name waxes as another wanes, but no type dies out entirely.

With the ample (though widely scattered) records of recent centuries available, changes in name popularity could be computed on a statistical basis. The results, however, would hardly justify the painstaking effort required. In a less laborious approach, yet yielding meaningful if rough data for one country, an area sample may be taken. Such a sample was taken for a portion of the eastern seaboard of the United States since the founding of the nation. The entries were examined on every fifth page of ship registers published for the ports of Boston and Charlestown, 1789–95;[1] New Bedford, Massachusetts, 1851–65; and New Bedford, 1866–1939.[2] While the first two samples covered six-year periods, the third covered a much longer period, although actually the entries fell preponderantly within the earlier years covered; that is, before New Bedford lost its standing as a maritime center. Each sample totaled from 100 to 200 names. For the present day there is no published list for a single port. Therefore a 178-name sample was taken from *MVUS68* by classifying the first entry on every fifth page. The results, expressed as percentages of each sample period, are shown in the table.

Ship name popularity for the United States (1789–1968) in percentages

Category	Boston-Charlestown 1789–95	New Bedford 1851–65	New Bedford 1866–1939	*MVUS68* 1968
Feminine first names	40	14.8	6.2	20
Feminine full names	0.9	10.9	16.2	1.1
Masculine first names	7.6	2.3	2.7	2.8
Masculine last or full names	5.7	24	25	8.5
First names of two persons	0.9	1.6	2.7	1.7
Place names	7.1	9.4	6.3	12
Christian and other religious names	0	0.8	0.9	1.1
Classical mythology names	9	3.9	3.6	1.1
Bird, fish, reptile, and other animal names	9	5.4	2.8	1.7
Names expressing success, fair play, industry	9.5	7.8	0	0
Miscellaneous	14.3	33.6	34	50

Assuming that the samples for the table were comparable for the different periods, interesting shifts in ship naming in the United States are evident.

Feminine first names were extremely popular 200 years ago, lost much popularity in the nineteenth century, and now have a popularity about half that of the early period. Feminine full names, not common in the beginning nor now, were quite popular in the nineteenth century. However, the total for feminine names of both types remained essentially constant at around 23 percent during the last three periods.

Masculine first names, never very popular, became less so between 1795 and 1851 and thereafter remained at a constant 2 to 3 percent level. However, masculine last names or full names, which became popular during the nineteenth century (as did feminine full names), have dropped to about the level of 200 years ago.

Place names are slightly more popular today than in earlier periods, but names from mythology have gone out of style (along, probably, with the decline in classical studies), and the same is true of animal names (bird, fish).

No names expressing industry and success appeared in the samplings after the Civil War, perhaps because of more corporate and less individual ownership of vessels, together with a gradually altered attitude toward hard work because of social security as a cushion against want.

The names classified as miscellaneous increased from 14 percent to a hefty 50 percent during the period studied. With one exception the miscellaneous names for all periods were similar. The exception was the many barge names consisting of letters and/or numerals; these appeared only in the latest sample and amounted to 27 percent of the miscellaneous names, or 13.5 percent of the total sample for the year 1968.

To see what data an English port would yield, a list of ships registered, built, or owned at Bristol between 1800 and 1838 was sampled,[3] although these years were not directly comparable with any of the American periods. The percentage count was as follows:

Feminine first names, 17.4; feminine full names, zero; masculine first names, 4.1; masculine full or last names, 15.3; first names of two persons, zero; place names, 19.4; Christian and other religious names, 1; classical mythology names, 16.3; animal (bird-fish) type names, 1; success names, zero; miscellaneous, 25.3

The principal difference was in the greater number of place and classical names than in the American samples.

A tabulation of names of American ships during periods from ten to about fifty years was made by William A. Fairburn.[4] He examined the names of 196 transatlantic square-rigged sailing packets in service out of New York during the years 1818–58 and classified them under the following headings by percent: geographical, 38.3; personal, 16.3; celebrities, 15.3; euphonious or pleasing, 8.2; historical, 6.1; national, 5.6; classical, 3.6; celestial and astronomical, 2.6; biblical, 2.0; and moral qualities, 2.0.

The next group Fairburn examined consisted of 447 American clippers and other fast ships of the 1850s, with the following results: euphonious or pleasing, 18.6; personal, 12.8; animals, including fish, bird, and insect,

10.1; mythical, classical, or imaginative, 8.9; connected with the sea, 8.1; geographical, 6.7; connected with the sky or wind, 6.5; worthy qualities, 5.8; astronomical, 5.0; historical celebrities, 4.5; sports, 4.2; races or men, 4.0; *golden*, 2.7; soldiers and sailors, 2.3. Fairburn noted that the discovery of gold in California and later Australia probably influenced the use of *golden* for twelve ships with such names as *Golden Age* and *Golden Dream*. *Eagle, ocean, pride, queen, sea,* and *star* formed part of many compound names, as they do today. Storm names were very popular, too, such as *Cyclone, Hurricane, Monsoon, Pampero,* and *Typhoon,* seemingly in defiance of elemental forces.

Finally, Fairburn considered the names of 242 Down Easters, square-riggers built for foreign trade and service around the Horn, from the decline of the clippers to the early twentieth century. He classified these names by percent as follows: men, 39.7; romantic (including some geographical, Indian, patriotic, and classical, but apparently selected for euphonious or emotional appeal), 36.8; geographical, 11.1; women, 7.0; saints, 5.5 The high percentage of person names for Down Easters was attributed in part to promotion efforts involved in share ownership. Often the largest subscriber could expect to have the ship named for him or one of the women in his life. Quite likely saints' names sometimes indirectly honored a relative or friend of an owner and perhaps had the additional advantage of appealing to foreign-born seamen during the period of heavy immigration from Ireland and Germany.

18. Ancient and Classical Divinities

The names of ancient and classical gods and goddesses constitute a persistent category of ship names throughout the ages. In lands of their origin and frequently in other places as well, these deities were for many centuries a serious consideration in nomenclature. Names of deities used in Egypt, Babylonia, and Rome have already been mentioned. Greeks certainly—and Phoenicians and others, probably—also used divinity names.

That the honoring and petitioning of the gods by mariners was customary is clear from the classics. Thucydides in his history of the Peloponnesian War (book 28) described the Athenian fleet with all aboard and about to sail: "At the herald's signal the customary prayers before sailing were pronounced, rising in unison from all the galleys as a single prayer. From end to end of the fleet captains and soldiers poured libations of wine from cups of silver and gold."

1. The container freighter *Margaret Johnson* has her stern name repainted by a seaman. To make this job easier for unskilled hands, the ship has letters of name and port cut from metal and tack-welded to the hull.

2. Large letters are used in the name of the British "roll-on roll-off" freighter *Dilkara*. Symbols at the bow near the waterline caution tugs and small craft that a bulbous portion of the hull projects ahead under water as a danger to propellers.

3. Name of the motor freighter *Icaros* appears on accommodation ladder. Nameboard can be seen atop pilothouse.

ごうるでん げいと ぶりっじ
神 戸
GOLDEN GATE BRIDGE
KOBE

4. Stern lettering in Japanese characters and Latin letters on the Japanese freighter *Golden Gate Bridge*.

5. Illuminated pilothouse nameboards in Latin letters and Chinese characters on the cargo-liner *Oriental Pearl*.

6. *Chapter Eleven* refers to a section of the law on bankruptcy, suggesting that enough money went into the yacht to leave the owner almost insolvent.

7. The yacht *Carita* displays her name and home port on carved wooden stern plaques.

8. The wide stern of *Golar Freeze* offers an excellent background for the name, which indicates a "reefer," or refrigerator ship.

9. Pilothouse nameboard of the *Export Courier*. Once such boards were handsomely carved by hand; now the letters are routed out by a power tool or simply painted on.

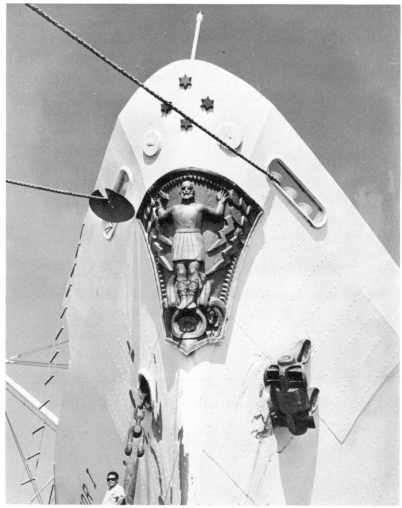

10. Cast metal prow emblem representing the god *Thor* on the freighter *Thor I*, a link with the old figurehead tradition.

11. Name of yacht *En Route* is shown on that vessel's portlight screen attached to shrouds.

12. Example of an extremely brief ship's name and the survival of an ancient deity name. Ea was the Babylonian god of wisdom and magic.

13. Large illuminated name of German passenger ship *Hamburg* atop the pilot-house.

Even after the advent of Christianity, although belief in the old protective divinities ceased, their names continued to be used and are used in significant numbers today, partly because of tradition and partly because of classical studies and the retelling of the old myths to children. Irrespective of what ship list is examined, from whatever Western nation, it will contain names of the old gods.

Four ship lists were analyzed for the occurrence of the names of about seventy of the more important gods and goddesses; of these an even fifty were found in use today or in British warship history. Names not found were principally those of Egyptian and Near Eastern origin; these names, however, might be found in local records or in forms not recognized. Compounds in which divinity names formed the second word were not sought out; in fact, no compounds of any sort were included except those with Thor, such as *Thorhild* (1956).

The four ship lists examined were: (I) *Lloyd's*, having over 47,000 entries for seagoing vessels of 100 tons or more (of which 312, or approximately two-thirds percent, were god-named); (II) *MVUS68*, having about 67,000 entries, including many small commercial craft and yachts of over five tons; (III) *BWN*, listing just over 2,200 British warship names covering four centuries; and (IV) *Jane's*, listing over 14,000 ships from 100 countries. The tally from these lists follows:

Egyptian: (I) 4 different gods for 4 different ships; (II) 3 gods for 6 ships; (III) 2 for 9; (IV) 1 for 1

Near Eastern, Crete: (I) 4 for 7; (II) 6 for 8; (III) 4 for 9; (IV) 3 for 3

Grecian: (I) 14 for 123; (II) 15 for 102; (III) 9 for 58; (IV) 9 for 17

Roman: (I) 13 for 97; (II) 9 for 60; (III) 10 for 110; (IV) 7 for 25

Norse-Germanic: (I) 5 for 82; (II) 6 for 33; (III) 1 for 5; (IV) 7 for 14

The names most frequently found, in descending order, were *Neptune*, *Thor*, *Venus*, *Poseidon*, *Jupiter*, *Minerva*, *Diana*, *Castor*, *Hermes*, and (with variations) *Odin*. Some of these have obvious associations with sailors and the sea.

Duplication of entries in *BWN* and *Jane's* was minimal. Although the use of *MVUS68* and *BWN* weighted the results in favor of American and British ships, naming frequency for the old gods was not greater for those nationalities. The tally from *Lloyd's* showed such names were just as popular in the other maritime nations, except in the Orient, and even Japan had a *Jupiter Maru* (1968). Not surprisingly the Norse-Germanic names in *Lloyd's* were commonest for ships from nations bordering the Baltic Sea.

The persistent popularity in modern times of classical gods' names may be inferred from the lists of seventeenth-century French, German, and Scandinavian men-of-war as published by the Society for Nautical Research. These old lists doubtless reflected the Renaissance interest in the classical past and almost completely ignored the northern gods.

19. Christian Names

Just as the ancients honored their gods, Christians of all nations have dedicated innumerable ships by name to God, to the Virgin Mary, to angels, and to saints.

At one time, religious observances took place several times daily aboard ships from Protestant as well as from Catholic countries. On Spanish ships the turning of the sand clock every half hour was accompanied by a religious reminder; for, as Samuel Eliot Morison observed, the ship depended for safety not only on her own staunchness and the seamen's skill but on the grace of God, and in the great days of sail, seamen were the most religious of all workers.[1] Many small craft today carry a plaque, usually cast in bronze, which reads: "O, God, Thy sea is so great and my ship is so small," and fishing boats often have shrines or, as in the not unique case of the large tuna clipper *Cape San Vincent* of San Juan, Puerto Rico, a tiny chapel. So it is not surprising that, past and present, religious names constitute a significant category.

English men-of-war have included *Christ* (1512), *Jesus of Lubeck* (1544), several called *Angel*, a Dutch prize *Maria Sancta* (1665), and many with saints' names.[2] Ships in the time of James I included *Blessing of God, Cherubim, Good God, Handywork of God, Seraphim, Spirito Sancto, Trinity,* and *Virgin*. There was also a *Golden Calf*.[3] In the last part of the nineteenth century a schooner out of Portmadoc, Wales, was called *Twelve Apostles*.[4]

English ship names also reflected divisions in the Christian world, such as *Reformation* (ca. 1650) and *Quaker* (ca. 1670).[5] *Anabaptist* sailed during the reign of James I.[6] In 1748 *Bethel*, of colonial Massachusetts, with only thirty-eight men aboard captured a Spanish treasure ship carrying 110 men.[7]

Since the Reformation, despite the many religious names in use in the English-speaking world, such names have been most popular in countries with largely Greek Catholic and Roman Catholic populations. At one time Spain required that every ship have a religious name, as did all five of Magellan's ships. Those Manila galleons, which for 250 years plied the Pacific between the Philippines and Acapulco, carried such names as translate into *Jesus and Mary, Rosary,* and *Our Lady of Life*.[8] The first ship built on the 2,500-mile coast stretching from Alaska to the tip of Lower California and then up the eastern side of that peninsula was *Triumph of the Cross* (1719) (*El Triunfo de la Cruz*). This *was* a triumph for the Jesuit Juan Ugarte, a man of many talents, who had to build a road ninety miles into the mountains of Lower California for timber before he could start to build. The vessel, with which Ugarte proved that California was not an island, was still in use in 1735.[9]

Old Testament names have never been widely used. The English captured the twenty-four-gun *Adam and Eve* from the Dutch in 1652 and retained the name; earlier they had a ship of the same name. In 1665 they had *Patriarch Isaac*, a prize flyboat.[10] Hamburg had a forty-eight-gun *Prophet Daniel* in 1649. *Noah's Ark* was a name borne by three seventeenth-century Danish-Norwegian warships. In the same century the name *King David* was used on Swedish, German, and Danish-Norwegian ships.[11] The Venetians had *David Goliath* and *Prophet Elijah*, galleys that engaged the Turks at the Dardanelles in 1655 and 1657, respectively.[12] Only a few Old Testament names appear in modern registers.

Today religious names are most widely used on craft owned by fishermen of Portuguese, Spanish, Italian, Greek, Yugoslavian, Central American, and South American ancestry in whatever country they may reside. However, as clippers grow larger, reaching multimillion-dollar lengths of over 200 feet and sail as far as Africa for tuna, the names tend to become *Star Clipper* or *Polaris* instead of *Saint Teresa* or *Restituta*.[13] Doubtless, in their powerful steel ships the fishermen find the sea less menacing than did the man alone or with several companions in a leaky wooden craft.

Nevertheless, religious names are still in wide use on large vessels throughout the world. *Lloyd's* listed 156 *Saint* as well as 123 *San* and 153 *Santa* ships. (Some, of course, refer not to saints directly but to places named for saints.) Together these 432 names constituted almost 1 percent of register entries. In addition, a quick inspection disclosed seven ships named *Trinity*, a Brazil tanker and a British fisherman called *Espiritu Santo*, thirteen names beginning with *Madre*, thirteen beginning with *Nuestra Senora*, and thirty-one beginning with *Virgen*. A French trawler was called *Regina Coeli* (1959); a Chilean bulk-wine carrier, *Concepcion* (1960); and a British trawler, *Galilean* (1959). There were a number of *Archangelos* as well as an *Angelic Protector* (1963) and others with the *Angelic* prefix. Finally, several pages of entries began with the Greek *Theo* for God (in some cases, part of person or place names). If all Christian names in *Lloyd's* were searched out, the total would doubtless exceed 1½ percent of all entries.

Such shortened titles for the Virgin Mary as the ship names *Concepcion* and *Restituta* reflect a common unofficial Spanish practice; for instance, the Manila galleon *Nuestra Senora de los Remedios* (ca. 1600) was simply called *Remedios*.[14] (For a very early use of *Mary*, see the section on "Feminine Names.")

20. Political Names

Numerous instances exist of ships named for political ends. Such names honor important individuals, allies, groups, areas, or countries or express discontent with political conditions or outright defiance of rulers. Political names may be tinged with ideological or religious concepts, may have the intention of influencing others, may echo a slogan or war cry, or may memorialize a significant date. The name may be that of a political agreement, a document, a party, or an ethnic leader; in the last instance the intent is less to honor the leader than to indicate adherence to his principles or to invite support from his followers. In short, a political name, has many aspects and may be a person name, a place name, a thing name, or an abstract name.

Fundamental challenges or changes in a nation's political life usually spawn political ship names. The naming may be a matter of official policy, as when *Edinburgh, Glasgow*, and *Union* in Queen Anne's reign marked the Act of Union of Scotland with England.[1] It may also be a spontaneous reaction by individuals supporting a cause, as happened in the American colonies with such names as *Bunker Hill, Concord*, and *Lexington*.[2] How the names of Royal Navy ships were changed during Cromwell's regime and then again during the Restoration is well covered in *BWN* and elsewhere. That political significance may survive long after actual events is illustrated by the naming of a sixteen-gun Massachusetts privateer *Oliver Cromwell* during the American Revolution.[3]

In the American Civil War a naming and renaming process occurred rather like that in Cromwell's day; and just as no British warship today honors Cromwell, so no American warship honors the leader of the South, although five Confederate craft once were called *Jeff Davis* or *Jefferson Davis*. One of these, a full-rigged brig built in 1845 and commissioned as a privateer in 1861, captured nine sail in seven weeks and was feared from Delaware to Maine.[4]

The period defined by the American Revolution affords numerous examples of political naming. *Defiance* (1765), a Massachusetts sloop, was launched in the same year that the Stamp Act was defied, and the name of the Philadelphia brig *Repeal* (1766) urged the repeal of that act. The Rhode Island sloop *Pitt* honored the Englishman who in 1766 had favored the colonies.[5] *Liberty* as early as 1768 expressed the desire of many colonists and was the name of John Hancock's sloop taken by British customs at Boston for smuggling Madeira wine.[6] Personifying a lovely goddess, *Liberty* appeared several dozen times as a ship name during the Revolutionary War and the troubled period on the high seas thereafter. Another poetic personification used even earlier on American ships was *Columbia*. Although both names are still popular, they have lost most of their impact.

In a list of 196 privately armed ships of Salem, Massachusetts, during the Revolution (ships with a total of 1,965 guns and 7,361 men), every seventh or eighth name reflected the war.[7] Besides *Bunker Hill, Lexington, Concord,* and *Oliver Cromwell* already mentioned, this list included *American Hero, Defense, Freedom, Marquis de la Fayette, Revolt, Retaliation, Revenge, Scourge, True American, Union, Washington,* and both *Junius* and *Junius Brutus* after the pseudonymous writer of a series of public letters criticizing public policy.

At the outbreak of hostilities the colony of Massachusetts launched the sloop *Tyrannicide* as a "state vessel of war."[8] *Rising States* of Boston, a privateer snow commissioned in late 1776, was another instance of revolutionary fervor; originally the British transport *Annabella,* she was retaken the following year.[9] *Rising States* continued to be a popular name in New England ports; at Newport, Rhode Island, there were fourteen entries for *Rising States* prior to 1811. *Rising Sun* signifying a political dawn was another popular name.[10] *Resistance* (1777) was a Connecticut brigantine and *Vengeance* (1779) a twelve-gun brig bought in France. In various ports a number of vessels were fitted out as *Washington* and as *Hancock,* and an armed galley from New York was *Lady Washington* (1776). In 1776 all the leading centers of revolt were indicated by name: *Virginia,* twenty-six-gun frigate; *Boston,* twenty-four-gun frigate; and *New York* and *Philadelphia,* each three-gun gundalows. Also there were *Congress* (1776), a twenty-eight-gun frigate; *Confederacy* (1778), a thirty-six-gun frigate captured by the British and renamed *Confederate;* and *Alliance* (1778), a thirty-two-gun frigate heralding support from France.[11] *Reprisal* carried Benjamin Franklin to France to solicit help for the colonies and later took English prizes into French ports in an effort to embroil England and France in war.[12]

The "Don't tread on me" slogan of the rattlesnake flag had its echo in the Salem privateer *Rattlesnake* commissioned in 1781. Captured that same year, she was renamed *Cormorant* until the Admiralty, discovering it already had a *Cormorant* in service, restored the name *Rattlesnake*, probably unaware of any revolutionary significance.[13]

After the formal peace of 1783 many aggressive names such as *Adamant* and *Fusileer* and *Freedom* continued in use, as shown by the Boston-Charleston register for 1789–95. However, most political ship names suggested the concerns of an emerging nation, for in addition to *Federal* and *Federalist* three ships were called *America* and eleven *Union*. By 1797 the frigate *United States* reflected an established nation, and the frigate *Constitution* commemorated the document adopted as the basic law of that nation.[14]

An instance in England of a ship named for a documented political agreement was the armed merchantman *Covenant of Hull* (ca. 1645).[15] Doubtless this referred to the Solemn League and Covenant in 1643 between Parliament and the Scots, agreeing among other things to preserve Presbyterianism as the Church of Scotland religion.

A political naming reflecting little credit on the United States involved the frigate *Crescent* (1797), given to Algiers but never mentioned in schoolbook accounts of how American ships in 1804 wiped out Algerian pirates. By treaty in 1795, in order to purchase immunity for American merchantmen, the United States agreed to pay the dey of Algiers one million dollars in cash and $21,000 annually in naval stores and to deliver a new frigate. To flatter the dey the secretary of war named the promised frigate *Crescent* after the emblem favored by the Moors.[16]

Despite the eventual bold suppression of the pirates, American ships were soon denied freedom of the seas by politics at home and conflict abroad. Opposed to one another in a continuing enmity, both England and France were seizing United States ships, a situation that Thomas Jefferson met with the Embargo Act, which prohibited United States ships from trading with the hostile nations and soon caused unemployment of about 50 percent in many seaports, while ships rotted at anchor. In one demonstration against this law, an old longboat named *O-Grab-Me* (*embargo* reversed), with sails unbent, rigging slack, and hull paint peeling, was loaded on a dray and dragged through the streets of Portland, Maine, followed by a band playing funeral dirges. At the center of town stirring speakers held the crowd while *O-Grab-Me* passed from sight behind a building to undergo a transformation, later emerging with hull painted, rigging trim, and sails bent. To the strains of martial music, the vessel was then navigated to the harbor and launched to represent what would happen with the embargo lifted.[17]

Washington eventually got the message, from many quarters; but the War of 1812 soon followed. This war produced another rash of political ship names. Among these were those of two New York privateers, *United We Stand* (which took sixteen prizes) and her running mate *Divided We Fall*.[18] Bristol, Rhode Island, sent out among others *Block-ade*, *Fourth of July*, and the most successful privateer of the war, the brigantine *Yankee*, which made six cruises and took forty-one prizes worth $3,000,000.[19]

Comparable to the quick transformation of *O-Grab-Me* were the deceptions said to have been perpetrated by Russia in recent years. Warships that left the Mediterranean for the Black Sea reportedly returned to the Mediterranean under different names for a fast "increase" in naval tonnage.

Sometime political naming is like the naming of a child for a rich uncle, a gambit used by petroleum companies with Middle Eastern interests. An earlier incident of this sort occurred in 1873 when the shah of Persia visited England. To flattter the shah and help counteract Russian influence, H.M.S. *Blonde* was hastily renamed *Shah*. On a tour of inspection, the shah's aide pointed out that the new name, in Persian characters on a plate suspended temporarily over the side, had beeen hung upside down.[20]

Ship names also honor ethnic groups. During the American Civil War authorities in the North wooed the Irish, who constituted about 40 percent of the foreign-born population, in one instance by christening a side-wheel double-ender *Shamrock* with a bottle of Irish whiskey on Saint Patrick's Day, 1863.[21] The South also wooed the Irish with *Saint Patrick* (1864), a submersible torpedo boat built at Mobile.[22] A similar intent prompted the assignment during World War II of the first Negro ever to command an American merchant vessel to *Booker T. Washington*, a Liberty ship named for that famous black man.[23] Also during World War II, when Latin American and South American solidarity was important, the United States named twelve Victory ships for such countries, and twenty Liberty ships received the names of *Simon Bolivar*, *Bernardo O'Higgins*, and other patriots.

21. Peace, Friendship, Diligence, Profit

Although many names have been born in strife, by contrast there have also been many expressing the desire for peace, friendship, diligence, and profitable trade.

The register for the port of New York between 1789 and 1867 showed no less than sixty-six entries for *Friendship* and thirty-four for *Olive Branch*.[1] In only six years at Boston and Charlestown, 1789–95, there were twenty-five entries for *Friendship* and also a Hingham schooner called *Harmless*.[2] While several of the *Friendship* entries may have been duplicated at the various ports, the name continued to be popular; sixteen ships of that name are listed today in *MVUS68*. *Love and Unity* (1803) was a brig from Dighton, Massachusetts.[3] *Amity* was the postwar name for one of the first packets of the Black Ball Line, which in 1818 became the first line in history known to have several vessels scheduled to sail in regular succession on specified dates between specified ports, in this instance between New York and Liverpool.[4] *Fellowship* and *Love Us All* traded in the reign of James I.[5]

Many names in lists and registers convey the idea of economic success and diligence in trade. *True Dealing, Trades Increase, Prosperous Joan, Treasure, Prosperity*, and *Merchants' Hope* were early instances in the time of James I.[6] One American register of the late eighteenth century showed these entries: *Active* (3), *Bee* (4), *Beaver* (4), *Commerce* (8), and *Industry* (28).[7] A few years later there were *Prompt*[8] and three entries for *Magnet*[9] in the hope, perhaps, of attracting dollars. *Emporium* (1832) of Boston suggests a cruising department store.[10]

Periods of difficulty in commerce were reflected in the christening in Rhode Island of a Bristol sloop *Hard Times* (1829) and the naming of a Weymouth sloop *Hardscrabble* (1850).[11]

In *Lloyd's* ship names expressing the diligence and success idea included *Prosperity* (1958), Singapore tanker; *Ever Success* (1969), Liberian freighter; *Prompt* (1969), Hamburg tug; and *Pronto* (1960), Helsinki tanker. *Oceanic Amity* (1944), *Oceanic Peace* (1962), *Grand Trust* (1961), and *Olivebranch* (1928) carried on the idea of peace and friendship for profit.

22. Feminine Names

Feminine names for American ships, as indicated previously, have averaged around 20 percent of total ship names since the middle of the nineteenth century, after having totaled as high as 40 percent when Washington was president.

Doubtless the popularity of particular feminine names for ships correlates with fashion in names among the general population. By way of illustration, *Sukey*, a diminutive for *Susan* or *Susanna*, had a brief two-continent popularity. *Sukey* appeared seven times in *Lloyd's* edition of

1776 as the name for ships, mostly brigs, built between 1759 and 1773. *Sukey* appeared in American registers between 1789 and 1795 but not thereafter. There were ten entries for *Sukey* in the registers at the ports of Boston-Charlestown, eight at New York, and two at Newport. Perhaps the name was that of a celebrated beauty of the age. Two young women called Sukey caught the eyes of British officers when troops landed at Boston in 1769.[1] The nephew of a Lord Ponsby saw Sukey Sheaffe, a Tory's daughter, watching from a balcony and exclaimed, "That girl seals my fate," which she did. The other marriage was that of Sukey Inman, from a Whig family, to the captain of *Beaver*, one of the ships involved in the Boston Tea Party. There is only the slimmest possibility that either of these belles loaned her name to American ships.

Certainly the all-time favorite feminine name for ships in English, and probably also throughout the Christian world, in one form or another, is *Mary*. In *MVUS68* this name appeared 34 times; additionally, in combination with a second given name or with a surname, it appeared 549 times. This frequency was slightly under 1 percent of total listings in the register. Other popular names in the same register included *Elizabeth* (84), the diminutives *Betty*, *Betsy*, and *Bessie* (229), *Helen* (148), and *Sally* (75). Quite likely *Elizabeth*, long a popular name, owes something to the English queens so named, while *Mary* without doubt is popular for girls directly or indirectly because of the Virgin Mary. Four Christian inscriptions found on the island of Siros in the Cyclades showed that *Mapia*, the transliterated New Testament form of *Mary*, appeared as a ship name very early in the Christian period.[2]

In the list of ships registered at New York, 1789–1867, *Mary* occurred 128 times as a single name and 392 times in combination (plus *Maria* 101 and 32 times), showing how much more popular on a percentage basis the name was then than now.[3] In the New York register *Sally* came next (139 and 41), then *Betsey* (122 and 16), *Eliza* (103 and 92), *Polly* (91 and 13), and *Elizabeth* (68 and 32). In that New York register other popular names, alone or in combination, included *Harriet* or *Harriot* (101), *Jane* (101), *Hannah* (52), *Frances* (47), and *Fanny* (38).

A note in *The Mariner's Mirror*, based on an examination of *Lloyd's* edition for 1895, listed the sixteen favorite feminine names in each of two categories, mercantile vessels and yachts.[4] *Mary* and *Elizabeth* predictably headed the mercantile list, but surprisingly neither appeared at all in the yacht list, which was headed by *Mabel*. Only *Florence* was duplicated on both lists, suggesting that traditional names are more likely to be carried by merchant vessels and currently popular names by yachts.

Colonial records of North Carolina (1767–68 and 1771–76) were

studied by Joseph Goldenberg, who found names of women dominating
the listings of 566 vessels. *Sally* (33) was most popular, followed by
Betsey (27) and *Nancy* (15).[5] One *Nancy*, a brig carrying contraband
from Baltimore to Curaçao in 1779 when taken by H.M.S. *Sparrow*,
probably would have been released for lack of evidence except for a fate-
ful coincidence.[6] *Nancy's* captain managed to drop overboard a packet
of incriminating documents that were subsequently produced in court.
A young lieutenant on another British ship caught a shark and found
Nancy's papers intact in its stomach.

The count for feminine first names in R. C. Anderson's list of 366
English men-of-war (1509–1649) was headed by *Mary* (17), followed by
Katherine (5), *Elizabeth* (4), *Barbara* (4), *Anne* (3), and others (8).[7]
Some of these names were qualified by *Great* or other words, but female
saints were not counted. These feminine names totaled forty-one, or
more than 10 percent; the same list, incidentally, had twenty masculine
first names. The reigns of Henry VIII (who had two wives named Kath-
arine), of Queens Mary and Elizabeth, and of James I (whose wife was
Anne of Denmark) all fell within the period of this list. Thus of the
popular names apparently only *Barbara* had no royal counterpart.

Of course, the names of women (as distinct from those of goddesses
and saints) had been in use for ships long before 1509. First, perhaps the
saint prefix was sometimes dropped, it being understood that the saint
was intended. Or perhaps the first names used were those of royal or
noble ladies, influencing merchant shipowners similarly to honor their
women. At any rate, various wool ships of the fifteenth century carried
such names as *Mary of London*.[8] A century earlier, Chaucer, who had
been in charge of wool customs for the port of London, described in
Canterbury Tales the hardy mariner whose ship was *Maudelayne*.

Feminine ship names have varied in popularity not only with time
but also in different places at the same time and even in the same country.
Thus, whereas *Abigail*, *Eliza*, and *Polly* were common in registers of the
eastern United States seaboard, New Orleans registers included more
names with French-Spanish flavor, such as *Dolores*, *Felicite*, and *Justine*.[9]

23. Masculine Names

Although the use of men's first names for ships is as old as the use of
women's first names, it has never been so popular. Linguistically, a feminine name seems more suitable. The words for watercraft in Greek and
Latin, most such words in Italian, some in French and German, and the

important *nave* in Spanish are all of feminine gender. At one time, knowledgeable Englishmen apparently distinguished in using *he* or *she* between types of ships, whether the type words were masculine or feminine in French. Less informed writers often used the pronouns without discrimination, even changing them in the same sentence. Now for several centuries it has been customary to refer to a vessel as *she*.

The difference in popularity between masculine and feminine personal names may also be accounted for by the seaman's life. Men usually go to sea without women, and feminine names are reminders of loved ones ashore. Seamen, moreover, ascribe certain feminine characteristics to ships. *Seaman's Bride* was the name of a number of ships, including a Maine sloop of 1854 and a Maryland schooner of 1856.[1] *Female* (1807) was the name of a letter-of-marque brig sailing out of Baltimore during the War of 1812.[2]

In the Anderson list of 1509–1649, cited in the previous section, there were eighteen masculine first names versus forty feminine ones. *Henry* appeared three times, referring in each case to the king, while *John* and *George* each occurred twice, and all the rest, once each.[3] The port of New York list, also cited in the previous section, showed *John* to be without rival for the years 1789 to 1867; it appeared 420 times alone or in combination with a surname or other given names.[4] This list was only hastily scanned for other popular names, which appeared to be *James*, *Joseph*, *William*, *Henry*, and *Edward*. *George* appeared 169 times alone or in combination (26 combined with *Washington*).

24. Place Names

A major name category, especially in modern times, is that of the geographical, or place, name. Such names date from earliest times. The first known ship name, *Praise of the Two Lands*, was a place name referring to Upper and Lower Egypt (also a political name). Other examples of ancient place names were the Greek galleys *Salaminia* and *Rome*, the latter being a special type in that it designated a nation so powerful that the word among the Greeks eventually meant power. *Rome* is an extreme instance of how place names often carry overtones of meaning. As noted previously, many Roman warships were named for rivers and other geographical features.

Place names appeared infrequently, however, in the Anderson lists of English men-of-war (including hired ships) from 1509 to 1700, despite an occasional listing of a town, a river, a castle, and ports suffixed to the regular name; a few names probably referred to noblemen rather than to places.

The sampling of American registers, as tabulated previously, suggests that place names constituted from 6 to 9 percent of total names between 1789 and 1939 and around 12 percent in 1968.

Today, however, judging by the Marine Exchange data reporting the American and foreign tankers and freighters entering the ports of Los Angeles and Long Beach, about 25 percent carry place names, many in compounds, such as *Oregon Bear* (1952) and *Delphic Miracle* (1961). (Both of these were listed in *Lloyd's,* as were other names mentioned to the end of this chapter unless otherwise noted.) Incidentally, the Marine Exchange data show that person names total only about 15 percent, leaving about 60 percent for thing names and abstract names.

Place names for ships include continents, nations, provinces, states, cities, mountains, oceans, lakes, rivers, capes, islands, and just about every other geographical feature that ever appeared on a map or that never actually appeared anywhere except on a map in the folk imagination of mankind, places as reflected by *Parnassos* (1965), Piraeus ore carrier; *Valhall* (1966), Norwegian bulk freighter; and *Atlantis II* (1963), Woods Hole, Massachusetts, oceanographic ship, one of six in Lloyd's bearing the name *Atlantis.*

Most place names are simple, such as *Canada* (1953) of Stockholm; *Mississippi* (1960), French freighter; and *San Francisco* (1963), Delaware container ship. But some are compounds, such as in *City of Antwerp* (1965) of Hamburg, *State of Junjab* (1962) of Bombay, *Port Brisbane* (1949) of London, and *Star of Mecca* (1937) of Saudi Arabia. In other instances the place indication is used as a modifier, as in *American Lark* (1969) of New York, *British Admiral* (1965) of London, *World Banner* (1958) of Monrovia, *Atlantic Trader* (1958) of Philadelphia, and *Hongkong Surety* (1955) of Monrovia.

Some place names are general—*Arctic, Dixie, Delta, Orient, Tropic,* and the like. They sometimes stand alone as a ship name; more often they are combined with other words. Planets and stars are places, too, and have long supplied ship names. Now with the moon a port of call, lunar geographical features will doubtless begin to appear as ship names.

Some modern ship names recall ancient cities and vanished civilizations, for example, *Acropolis* (1932) a Piraeus passenger vessel, *Illiria* (1962) a Venetian freighter, *Pompeii* (1945) an Italian craft, *Angkor* (1954) a French tanker, and *Knossos* (1953) a Greek fish-factory ship.

Place names for naval ships, especially during a rapid expansion of wartime tonnage, including merchant bottoms, serve to focus interest on the national effort and elicit financial support. Giving a ship a place name is a gracious if cheap way of recognizing areas particular rulers might want to thank or influence. A ship named for a living man ordinarily flatters only one man, but a ship named for a city may interest a million or more persons. While the ship place name was not a significant category in colonial America, with the need for political and financial support during the Revolutionary War, warships soon were launched bearing the names of leading American cities. In recognition of Australian support in the Pacific during World War II, a cruiser was christened *Canberra*, the first time a foreign city was so honored by the United States Navy.[1]

Certain place names, such as those of battles, carry overtones of glory and appear not only on naval vessels but also on merchant ships; for example, *Thermopylae* (1949), Norwegian freighter; *Trafalgar* (1949), Tönsberg vegetable-oil tanker; and *Valley Forge* (1966), Wilmington, Delaware, tanker.

Often a city or country is indicated indirectly by a world-famous feature associated with it, for instance, *Champs Elysées* (1960), Dunkirk tanker; *Parthenon* (1960), Dutch freighter; *Golden Gate Bridge* (1968), Kobe container ship; and *Statue of Liberty* (1954), Liberian tanker.

Other times a place may be indicated by a nickname: Arizona, *Copper State* (1943); Vermont, *Green Mountain State* (1945); Pennsylvania, *Keystoner* (1953); Portland, Oregon, *Rose City* (1944).

Some place names for ships memorialize the birthplace or hometown of shipowners. *Balclutha* (1886), the square-rigged merchantman preserved at San Francisco, was named in Gaelic for Dumbarton, Scotland, home of her original owner.[2] A place name also may link a ship with a particular port, even with two ports as in the case of *Wilmington and Liverpool Packet* (1815), a Connecticut-built ship that solicited transatlantic custom.[3] Use of a port name as a ship name is really an invitation to shippers or passengers to think of the ship in connection with cargo or passage to that port. It also tends to solicit the goodwill of authorities and shippers in the port. More often than not the port name is an indication neither of nationality nor of registry, as may be true for other kinds of place names, as suggested by examples previously cited.

25. Abstract Names

Names of ships may be classified as concrete or abstract, according to their denotation or explicit meaning (as distinguished from connotation or associated meaning).

Naturalist (1945) is simply concrete; *American Legion* (1968), collectively concrete; *Mina D'Amico* (1954), uniquely concrete; *Atlantic Trader* (1958), generally concrete. (These names and those that follow, unless otherwise indicated, come from *Lloyd's*.)

Abstract names, on the other hand, convey a quality apart from any material object. *Grand Integrity* (1950) expresses the possession of a quality and is *positively* abstract. *Isn't*, borne in 1967 by a twelve-ton New York passenger craft, expresses lack of quality and is a rare example of a *negatively* abstract name.[1]

Such an old name as *Queen* is *relatively* abstract, since the meaning depends upon the existence of a relationship to a king or to subjects. A *nonrelatively* abstract name would be *Signality* (1937), coined for a 487-ton London vessel that presumably was remarkable.

Greek galleys, as has been indicated, had such abstract names as *Audacious, Glory, Charming,* and *Frivolous;* after all, the Greeks were masters of abstract thought.[2] The earlier Egyptians were more circumscribed by the concrete and did little more than combine the abstract with the concrete in such names as *Mighty Is Isesi*[3] or *Loved by Amon.*[4] The Anderson lists included *Speedwell* (1560), *Aid* (1562), *Revenge* (1577), *Desire* (1616), and *Dainty* (1645).[5]

Apparently abstract names are on the increase, perhaps because each century produces vessels in larger numbers to be given names. At any rate, a great many abstract names are found on the seas today, for example: *Atonality* (1950), British tanker; *Brilliance* (1949), Liberian tanker; *Comfort* (1941), Taiwan freighter; *Fidelity* (1953), Liberian tanker; and *Sagacity* (1946) and *Severity* (1954), both of London.

26. Naval Names

In navies tradition encourages the perpetuation of ship names. When the 100-foot *Karano*, built in A.D. 274 as the first Japanese vessel of note, was condemned after twenty-six years of service, the emperor issued a rescript: "Shall we not keep the name of that ship from being lost and hand it down to after ages?"[1] How long *Karano* was memorialized is not known—not, at any rate, to the time of World War II. In the British and American navies, however, some names from the earliest periods have been kept continuously active.

On the subject of naval names a number of excellent works are obtainable. For the Royal Navy these include *Ships of the Royal Navy: An Historical Index*[2] and *British Warship Names* (*BWN*), as well as several earlier works. There are also the men-of-war lists (*Lists 5* and *List 7*), as published by the Society for Nautical Research in England, and that society's lecture on ship names delivered in 1957.[3] Books for the United States include *Dictionary of American Naval Fighting Ships* (DANFS), being issued in successive volumes by the Navy Department (volume 2 including a section on the Confederate Navy); *Ship Names of the United States Navy*;[4] and the four-volume series titled *Ships of the United States Navy and Their Sponsors*.[5] There is also, of course, the invaluable series *Jane's Fighting Ships*, which groups modern naval vessels of all countries by type and class, so that naming patterns are discernible.

Although much of exceptional interest could be drawn from the afore-mentioned references, this temptation will for the most part be resisted, so as not to cover sketchily what these works offer in detail.

With respect to the United States Coast Guard, however, its naming practice is less well documented. Thus, information to me in a letter dated in May of 1970 from Captain T. McDonald, chief, Public Information Division, U.S.C.G., may be of interest here.

Essentially, the naming of cutters falls under the jurisdiction of our Office of Operations. Details are handled by one of their divisions having control over a particular class of cutter. For example, the Aids to Navigation Division would be responsible for all buoy tenders. A board of officers is selected to make recommendations to the Commandant, who has the final authority. As a matter of interest, we do take a great deal of pride in our history, and this is reflected in our continuing to carry on the names of former Coast Guard cutters. This is especially true with respect to cutters named for former Secretaries of the Treasury.

McDonald then listed Coast Guard vessels by class; this list, slightly abridged to give just one name example of each type, follows:

High-endurance cutters (378-foot), for former secretaries of the treasury (*Hamilton*) and Coast Guard heroes (*Jarvis*)

High-endurance cutters (327-foot), for former secretaries of the treasury (*Bibb*)

High-endurance cutters (311-foot), for former secretaries of the treasury (*Gresham*) and bays, straits, and inlets (*Cook Inlet*)

Icebreakers (polar), for winds (*Northwind*) and several with retained United States Navy names (*Staten Island*)

Icebreaker (Great Lakes), one, *Mackinaw*, for straits thereof

Medium-endurance cutters (210-foot), for desirable human traits (*Confidence*)

Oceangoing tugs, for Indian tribes and places (*Cherokee*)

Patrol craft (large), for capes (*Cape Hatteras*)

Patrol craft (small), for points (*Point Bonita*)
Harbor tugs (medium), for Indian tribes (*Apalachee*)
Harbor tugs (small), for marlinspike seamanship terms (*Towline*)
Buoy tenders (seagoing), for flowers, shrubs, trees (*Balsam*).
Buoy tenders (inland, large and small), for flowers, shrubs, trees (*Bluebell*)
Buoy tenders (inland, construction), for tools (*Sledge*)
Buoy tenders (river, large), for trees (*Dogwood*)
Buoy tenders (river, small), for Indian tribes (*Chippewa*) and shrubs (*Lantana*)

During the great naval expansion occurring during a war, the suitable naming of ships becomes a problem, as indicated by *BWN* in the discussion of British naming during World War II. An amusing account of ship naming during the same war was written by Captain William T. Calkins, USNR, who served under the chief of naval personnel, the officer who traditionally has the naming responsibility for the United States Navy.[6] Utilizing some of the names chosen, Calkins wrote: "The *Project* got out of *Control* when a *Knave* with an *Astute* and *Lucid* mind reached the *Pinnacle* of *Fancy* with his *Incredible* choice of the name *Fixity*."

Calkins went on to confess: "What it occasionally cost the Navy to burnish the names off all the equipment on a ship when I had goofed and had to rename her hurriedly, I'll never know." In that era of quick expansion, he had to avoid names already in use by allied naval and commercial vessels and names with a possible double entendre. Even reaching into the heavens was not safe, as he discovered when he almost named one ship after a star an astronomer had named for the poodle of his mistress.

What he called the "just-word" names were among the hardest to select, as for the score or more hospital ships. "Just try," he wrote, "to think of comfortable words that describe the idea of 'solace' or 'tranquility' as few as twenty times, using a new word each time."

Fish names for submarines, probably caused the most trouble. The navy had nearly 500 submarines afloat or abuilding. "The reasonable names like *Trout, Bass, Salmon,* and *Shark* were used up long before I appeared," Calkins noted. "I was reduced to scrabbling around for names like *Spinax, Irex, Merd,* and *Sirago*." Many fish with unpronounceable Latin names have no common names. Among common names are such unsuitable ones as blue-eyed scad. He named one submarine *Trepang* only to discover too late that the trepang is a sea slug. In desperation he finally arranged with several ichthyologists at the National Museum to assign English names that he had selected as being suitable for submarines, to subspecies of fish that previously had borne only scientific names.

Calkins had only naval names to worry about. Even more names were required for the thousands of freighters and tankers. Apart from fighting ships, the United States during World War II produced over 2,600 standard Liberty ships plus numerous Liberty hulls converted to special types, about 531 Victory ships, 536 T-2 tankers, 21 T-3 tankers, 74 C-4 types mostly transports, 64 S-4 combat transports, 50 seagoing tugs, and hundreds of special craft.

How Edith Bolling Wilson, wife of the American president, labored to name most of the ships launched by the United States Shipping Board during World War I is covered in the section "Some Famous Namers." She selected many Indian names. Some of these, hard to spell and hard to pronounce, were scorned by the press, such names as *Skunkscut, Shickshinny, Tobesofka*, and *Sisladobsis*.[7]

For merchant ships built during World War II the Maritime Administration followed a definite naming pattern for most vessels of certain types.[8] Thus, C1 cargo ships were named for capes (*Cape Cod*), C2 ships for famous clippers (*Lightning*), C3 ships for fish, birds, or other animals with the prefix *Sea* (*Sea Wren*), and C4 ships for fish, birds, or other animals with the prefix *Marine* (*Marine Lynx*). T1 coastal tankers carried the names of major United States oil fields (*Benton Field*); T2 tankers, the names of American battles, national parks or monuments, or historical sites (*Mission Purisima*). Liberty ships received the names of persons considered to have made notable contributions to American history or culture (*Jack London*) and of merchant seamen who had lost their lives in service. Liberty colliers were named for major seams of coal (*La Salle Seam*). Victory ships had the word *Victory* following the name of an allied country (*Britain Victory*) or the name of a United States city or town. Mariner class C4-S-la vessels had such names as *Freestate Mariner*.

About 200 liberty ships loaned to the British all had names with the prefix *Sam*. It was widely supposed that this came from Uncle Sam. Actually it was a British acronym: Superstructure Aft of Midship.[9]

27. Naval Trophy Names

Warships sometimes have trophy names.[1] Strictly speaking, such a name is that of an enemy prize, often won in an exceptional display of valor and taken into the victorious navy without a name change. By extension, trophy names include those of successive warships carrying on the original trophy name. Sometimes the trophy name commemorates a victory where the enemy ship was sunk rather than taken.

A good example of this process is provided by *Formidable*, a historic British naval name. This name was retained for the French flagship captured by Edward Hawke in 1759. Sailing in the second British *Formidable* (1777) as his flagship, George Rodney added glory to the name in engagements against the French, culminating in the defeat of Comte de Grasse in 1782. Subsequently, three more major British ships were called *Formidable*, the last two being the battleship of 1898 sunk in World War I and the carrier of 1939 sold after World War II. Doubtless the name will be used again.

Boxer is an example of a United States trophy name. The fourteen-gun British brig *Boxer* struck her colors to *Enterprise* off the Maine coast in 1813 but was not taken into the navy. The name, however, became that of a fourteen-gun brig launched in 1815; then it went successively in 1831 to a ten-gun schooner (later a brig), in 1865 to a captured blockade runner formerly called *Tristram Shandy*, in 1904 to a brigantine that became a training vessel at Annapolis, and in 1944 to a carrier that won eight battle stars for service in the Korean War. Although the name was stricken with the decommissioning of the carrier in 1969, it will almost certainly be carried on.

Another United States trophy name is *Peacock*, recalling the nine-gun British vessel sunk by the ten-gun *Hornet* in 1813. The next year saw the launching of an American warship with this name, which is carried today by a coastal minesweeper. Other United States names from British vessels taken or sunk long ago include *Jason*, 1943 repair ship, and *Savage*, 1943 radar picket ship. Both *Finch* and *Fox* were defeated British vessels whose names are still in use. However, the second *Finch*, the destroyer of that name, was really named for an ensign killed in 1942; and the third, fourth, and fifth (present) *Fox* (1964 guided-missile frigate) were actually named for Lincoln's assistant navy secretary. The name of the aircraft carrier *Tripoli* originally was a trophy name from the Barbary States.

The Royal Navy perpetuated numerous trophy names, mostly from ships taken during the long naval hostilities with France but also from such American ships as *Chesapeake* (1799) thirty-six-gun frigate (two successors) and *Raleigh* (1776) thirty-two guns (five successors).

Enterprise has been used by two nations as a trophy name. In 1705 the British captured the sixth-rate French *Enterprise* and later reassigned the name to five successor vessels, including an inshore-survey craft of today. In 1775 the American colonists took the ten-gun British *Enterprise*.

This introduced the name into the United States Navy where, with a proud history, it presently is carried by a nuclear-powered attack carrier.

Names of sea battles may constitute a borderline type of trophy name. Thus the United States presently has carriers called *Coral Sea* (1946) and *Midway* (1945). The Royal Navy has had four warships called *Trafalgar*, the first a first-rate ship of 1820 and the last a destroyer of 1944.

28. Duplicated Warship Names

Trophy naming is one reason for names' being duplicated on warships of different nations, particularly Great Britain, France, and the United States. Some duplication occurs because of the strong impetus to pass on earlier names to new ships. Even though a ship is lost to an enemy, the feeling is strong among professional men that honorable defeat does not disgrace a name. Another reason for duplications is simply that certain names are part of the common heritage of several nations or of Western man.[1]

Sometimes ships with the same name are on opposite sides at the same time. Warships at Trafalgar in 1805 included on the British side a *Neptune* (98 guns) and on the opposite side a French *Neptune* and a Spanish *Neptuno*, as well as a British *Swiftsure* (74 guns) and a French *Swiftsure* (74 guns). Others with duplicated names were the French *Argonaute* (74 guns) and the Spanish *Argonauta* (80 guns).[2]

The maritime heritage of the United States definitely came from England. Thus in ship naming there are many duplications. The British navy has had at least six *Essex* ships, excluding hired vessels. The first in 1653 honored Cromwell's general, the third Earl of Essex; after the Restoration the *Essex* name continued but was considered geographical in origin. The first American *Essex* (1799) celebrated a county or town of Massachusetts, which like numerous other places in the former colonies had the English maritime center as a name source. The frigate *Essex* took many British prizes in the War of 1812 until captured in 1814 at Valparaiso and taken into the Royal Navy under the same name. The last British *Essex* (1901) was a cruiser, sold in 1921. The United States, after having the ironclad steamer *Essex* (1861)—which was a screw steamer constructed of wood, with a long naval history from 1876 to 1930—had the aircraft carrier *Essex* (1942), which won thirteen battle stars in World War II and four in the Korean War.

Hornet is another name common to the two navies. The first British *Hornet* was a sloop of 1745, which was followed by a cutter of 1763, a sloop of 1776, a sloop of 1794, another sloop of 1864, and destroyers of

1893 and 1911. The United States Navy has had eight *Hornet*s. The first was a merchant ship chartered in 1775 to serve in the first American fleet, which left in February of 1776 to raid the Bahamas. Recent ships with the *Hornet* name have been the 1940 carrier, which won four battle stars before being sunk in the Pacific in 1943, and her successor of 1943, which won seven battle stars and served in Vietnamese waters.

Mentioned previously as American trophy names, *Boxer, Fox, Jason, Peacock,* and *Savage* also continued active in the British navy. Among other duplications over the years in the two navies may be mentioned *Raleigh, Ranger, Vixen,* and *Wasp.*

Duplications are by no means limited to warships of the United States and the United Kingdom. Some years ago contributors to *The Mariner's Mirror* produced lists of person names duplicated in modern times in two or more navies.[3] Ships from Argentina, Austria, Canada, Chili, Denmark, France, Germany, Great Britain, Holland, Italy, Norway, Russia, Sweden, and the United States were represented. Person names included Archimedes, Champlain, Cochrane, Columbus, Dandolo, Don Juan of Austria, Duke of Edinburgh, Ericsson, Farragut, Franklin, Fulton, Galileo, Garibaldi, Magellan, Montcalm, Prince Eugene, Stonewall Jackson, Tordenskjold, Washington, Watt, and Volta.

In *Jane's* for 1970–71 only four person names were duplicated, and of those three quite likely were of persons just happening to have the same surnames. The fourth was *Mahan*, for the American naval strategist, carried by an Iranian patrol craft and a United States guided-missile frigate.

A total of 140 nonperson warship names, from a *Jane's* index of about 1,550 different ships, were duplicated two or more times. Heading the list were thirty-one names from mythology, followed by nineteen for stars or constellations, fifteen for places, fourteen abstract names, eleven for birds, and nine for mammals. Ships from Germany, Holland, Denmark, Norway, Sweden, Poland, Portugal, Israel, and the United States all were called *Delfin* or *Dolphin. Castor* appeared on warships of eight nations; *Orion* and *Vega* on seven; *Albatross* and *Rigel* and *Triton* on six; and *Diana, Jupiter, Pelican,* and *Regulus* on five. These duplications were principally on vessels of lesser importance, at least in the instance of the major powers.

29. Titles—Noble and Otherwise

Some of the earliest known English ship names were titles, such as *Queen. Lloyd's* disclosed the continuing popularity of titles—royal, noble, official, military, religious, polite—as names or more frequently as part of names. *President* and *Presidente* occurred in sixty-one such entries, *King* forty, *Queen* twenty-five, *Prince* or *Prins* twenty-six, and *Princess* or its variations forty-four. *Lord* appeared twenty-seven times and *Lady* eighty, *Don* fifty-seven and *Dona* forty-one, *Sir* forty-two, *General* thirty-eight, *Admiral* eighteen, and *Captain* thirty-two plus twenty-one *Kapitan* and variations. Others of which one to fifteen examples each were found included *Amiral, Archon, Baron, Cardinal, Chevalier, Commandante, Comte, Comtesse, Conde, Contessa, Consul, Countess, Duke, Earl, Emperador, Empress, Governor, Grand Count, Grande, Infante, Laird, Maharaja, Maharani, Marshal, Master, Miss, Pasha, Rajah, Senator, Senhora* and *Senora, Senhor* and *Senor, Sheikh, Sri, Sultan, Sultana,* and *Viscount. Professor* was popular in Russia.

All told, ships with the titles enumerated totaled 691, or approximately 1½ percent of *Lloyd's* entries. This tally ignored entirely the large number of ship names where the title appeared as a suffix, as in *Lancastrian Prince* (1969).

The percentage of title names in *MVUS68* was much higher. There were approximately 1,100 names from *Miss Abel* to *Miss Yvonne*, about 350 from *Lady Ada* to *Lady Zella*, and about 650 from *Captain Abdon* to *Captain Zip*. Most *captain* names appear on fishing craft or small passenger vessels and may be intended to advertise by identification, a survival of the tendency to identify a ship by owner or captain. Just those three titles—*Miss, Lady,* and *Captain*—totaled about 2,100, which was over 3 percent of *MVUS68* entries.

The regalia of royalty—that is, the crown, the globe, the key, the scepter, the sword, and the standard—have been rather widely used through history. Although frequently found alone, such names also appeared in compounds, as in Sweden's *Key of the Realm* (about 1628) and *Orb of the Realm* (about 1676). The wrecks of both these vessels were located off the Swedish coast.[1]

Akin to titles applied to persons are personifications or symbolic titles of nations, which are akin to both political and place names. These frequently have appeared on transoms, including *Columbia, Uncle Sam, Yankee*; also *Albion, Britannia, John Bull*; likewise *Shamrock, Thistle, Maple Leaf,* and *Marianne.* Oddly enough, such names often appear on ships from countries to which they do not pertain. Perhaps the usage is flattery to invite trade, perhaps a nostalgic gesture by "exiles." Two such names were merged in *Yankcanuck* (1963), Sault Sainte Marie cargo carrier operating on the Great Lakes. Another example was *Red, White, and Blue,* a ship-rigged metal lifeboat of 2.38 tons register, which in 1866 crossed the Atlantic in thirty-three days with two men and a dog. With no precedent in those days for such a crossing, Captain William Hudson's claim was widely disbelieved at the time.[2]

30. Heroes and Heroines

Many ship names commemorate heroes of legend or history, persons admired for courage, nobility, or exploits, especially in war.

For some legendary figures *Lloyd's* showed multiple entries, such as for *Achilles, Hector,* and *Ulysses. Roland* and other heroes of semilegend were there, including *King Arthur* and *Robin Hood.* Historical names were numerous, Admiral Nelson's more than once, also *John Paul Jones.* After man first walked on the moon, a large Piraeus tanker was renamed *Neil Armstrong* (1960).

MVUS68 listed the names of several of America's larger-than-life folk heroes. A decked barge recalled the fabulous logger *Paul Bunyan,* and, appropriately, a powerful Mississippi towboat was named for the black strongman *John Henry.* The register also had names of actual heroes, such as *Davy Crockett. Robert E. Lee* was commemorated by five watercraft.

The first ship ever named for General Lee made a legendary reputation carrying cotton and gold through the Union blockade until finally captured after twenty-one voyages; built on the Clyde in 1862, she was a schooner-rigged, iron-hulled paddlesteamer.[1] Today Lee is widely admired for his noble character, but an incident that occurred soon after the Civil War recalls that for a long while he remained strictly a Southern hero. When the famed Mississippi paddlewheeler *Robert E. Lee* (1868)—which later outraced the sixth steamer under the same owner to be called *Natchez* (1869)—approached completion at New Albany, Indiana, the Northern workmen, upon discovering the name that their handiwork was to carry, indignantly walked off the job. Nothing daunted, the owners towed her across the Ohio River to the Southern state of Kentucky for completion.[2]

Simply *Hero* (1800) was the name of a forty-seven foot shallow draft coastal sloop that made an incredible voyage in 1820 under Nat Palmer to islands rumored to lie off South America's tip and now known as the South Shetland Islands. Palmer's mission was to discover seal fisheries by trailing other vessels to the secret grounds. In doing so he became the first man known to have had a close look at the Antarctic continent, although he is not credited with its discovery since he did not go ashore.[3]

As for heroines, if the romantic Heloise types are eliminated, only a limited number of ships were named for heroines with demonstrated courage. To be sure, many names of the early Christian martyrs who displayed heroic virtue are found on ships today, although relatively few are on large ships of English-speaking nations. One authentic heroine does stand out as both a religious and a secular figure, the patron saint of France; her name was given to the French aircraft carrier *Jeanne d'Arc* (1961) and also to a Panamanian freighter, *Joan d'Arc* (1946).[4]

The story of another heroine, this one directly associated with the sea, has all the elements of great danger overcome by pluck and determination. Grace Darling was the daughter of the keeper of the Longstone light in the Farne Islands off Northumberland, England. During a fierce storm in 1838 the 192-ton steam packet *Forfarshire* came to grief on rocks near the light. Grace, then twenty-three years of age, went to the rescue with her father in a small boat. She handled one oar, her father two, on their mile-long struggle through crashing seas to reach survivors clinging to a wave-washed rock. Of the sixty-three persons originally aboard, the Darlings eventually rescued eight. Also surviving were eight crewmen who had lowered away in the only lifeboat before *Forfarshire* broke up, leaving passengers to their fate. The girl's bravery made her an international heroine. Wordsworth and Swinburne celebrated her in verse and artists on canvas. Queen Victoria and others sent medals and donations. A "Grace Darling Song" crossed the waters to America, where a number of vessels have carried her name.[5]

Probably the first American *Grace Darling* (1847) was a schooner out of Warren, Rhode Island.[6] In 1854 a clipper bearing the same name was launched and was considered a lucky ship. Sailors called her *Darling*. The sailing card announcing the Boston-to-San Francisco passage for this *Grace Darling*, May 19, 1864, depicts the heroine in flowing garments (certainly inappropriate for handling an oar), standing on a wave-splattered rock, with the lighthouse in the background and a coble already in the water nearby.[7] The coble actually used is preserved with other relics at the Grace Darling Museum in Northumberland.

The aforementioned schooner and clipper were not the only ones in the United States with the name. In 1916 a seven-ton Annapolis freighter was named *Grace Darling*, perhaps not after the heroine directly but after the former clipper ship, because many vessels have been named for the beautiful ships that made so many record passages.[8]

One of these clippers produced an all-but-forgotten American heroine, Mary Patten. Apparently one and perhaps two vessels memorialized her. Quite likely the schooner *Mary Patten*, launched 1864 in Brewer, Maine, was named for her.[9] Another *Mary Patten* (1943), a Liberty ship built at Richmond, California, carried the heroine's name.[10] (A different Mary Patten was the namesake for a Perth Amboy steam packet of 1893.) Married at sixteen, Mary went to sea with her husband and learned navigation as a pastime. On one passage in 1856 in *Neptune's Car* (1853) from New York to San Francisco, Captain Patten, having put his chief officer under arrest soon after sailing, collapsed from exposure and "brain fever" off Cape Horn and became blind. The second mate knew nothing of navigation. So Mrs. Patten, then aged nineteen, took command for fifty-two days and successfully brought *Neptune's Car* into San Francisco.[11] Word of this feat preceded the return of the ship to the East Coast, and Mrs. Patten was feted on arrival; but she, whose husband soon died in Boston, had little interest in being a glowing symbol for the early women's liberation advocates of that city.

As a variation in naming ships for heroes (and others as well), a descriptive appellative is sometimes used instead of the person's actual name. Donald McKay's medium clipper *Defender* (1855) honored Daniel Webster, as did a Medford-built vessel *Expounder* (1856).[12] A gracious instance of this sort of naming involved Admiral John Jervis, afterward the earl of St Vincent. Following an attack on Martinique in 1794, Jervis paid immediate tribute to a brave subordinate, Lieutenant Robert Faulkner, commanding the sloop *Zebra* (1780), by whose courage the French frigate *Royaliste* had been captured. "I have ordered her to be taken into our service," the Admiral declared, "and here is your commission to command her in which I have named her after yourself, sir, the *Undaunted*."[13] Although this prize was sold the following year, the name has since been carried by nine Royal Navy vessels.

31. Double Names

Many ships have carried the names of two persons, such as the British royal yacht *Victoria and Albert*. An earlier queen put her husband's name first on the new 500-ton warship, *Philip and Mary*, that she sent in 1557 to bring Philip of Spain to England and, she vainly hoped, to a life together.[1] At one time double names of this type were quite common. In a list of twenty-two English ships in 1654, five had such names, each name being composed either of two masculine or of two feminine names.[2]

The name popularity chart in the section on "Name Popularity" shows that the use of personal names as doublets has varied in the United States from just under 1 percent when the nation was founded, to an intermediate high of 2.7 percent, to about 1.7 percent today.

Obviously, most doublets are the names of co-owners, if not of owner and wife, owner and child, wife and child, two children, or the owner's parents. In at least one known instance a ship name, seemingly the full name of a man, actually was a concealed double name. This was *H. F. Bolt* (1876), a British trading ketch named for Harriet and Florence Bolt, daughters of the owner. This vessel, incidentally, which lasted until World War II, was the last trading ketch to remain active without auxiliary power.[3]

A double-name of a different type—one of the longest ship names likely to be encountered—was given by Alexander Patillo about 1821 to his Nova Scotia coaster *Lily of the Valley and Bear of the Sea*.[4]

32. Family Names

The use on ships of a family member's full name—as distinct from the owner's name—probably originated, in English, about the time surnames became common. Masculine full names cannot be distinguished from owner names, but since few women have been shipowners, it is reasonable to assume that a feminine name is probably of the family name type.

An early example of a ship named for a family member was *Margaret Cely* of London, by which George and Richard Cely, wool merchants, honored their mother about 1480.[1]

In recent years family names of both sexes have been displayed round the world by a number of shipping firms, particularly on the forty-eight Lykes Line vessels, from *Adabelle Lykes* (1963) to *Zoella Lykes* (1960), and the approximately eighty-five ships of the A. P. Möller line of Copenhagen, *Albert Maersk* (1958) to *Vibeke Maersk* (1948).[2] All the Möller freighters I have seen have been painted light blue with their names in very large black letters along the sides. These Lykes and Maersk names are also examples of series naming.

33. Consanguinity Names

What might be called the consanguinity name is illustrated by *Two Brothers, Three Sisters, Four Sons*, and *Five Daughters*. In various combinations of number and person, these names appeared in almost every American ship register. In *MVUS68* were eighty ships with names specifying three to seven sisters, brothers, sons, or daughters. The register for New York listed a brig in 1816 named *Twin Sons,* while that for Barnstable, Massachusetts, listed a sloop of 1804 called *Ten Sisters.*[1] (However, of the various *Seven Sisters,* several may have been named for the Pleiades constellation.)

Similar to the foregoing were the numerous other names in American lists suggesting relationships, such as *Two Marys, Three Josephs, Four Cousins,* and *Five Kids.* The aforementioned New York register had fourteen listings with *Uncle* in the name. Perhaps some of these honored uncles provided purchase money, as somebody must have done for the New York schooner *Generous Friend* (1800).

A Great Lakes schooner called *Our Son* was named and launched in sadness a few days after the drowning of the owner's son, about 1882, and was the last of the old sailing vessels on the Lakes when she foundered in 1930.[2]

34. Type Names

In more than one marina will be found pleasure craft simply called *Boat.* Such a type name may be a satiric comment on yacht naming or merely an attempt to attract attention. Nautical history, at any rate, discloses quite a few examples of type names. In 1779 two Jamaica merchants called their privateer *Ballahou,* the technical term for a type of fast schooner.[1] *Pink* of Edgartown was registered at Plymouth, Massachusetts, in 1810.[2] *The Steamboat* was what John Fitch called his pioneer steamer, which made regular runs at six miles an hour on the Schuylkill in Pennsylvania as early as 1790.[3] And *The Steamboat* was what Robert Fulton first called his successful creation seventeen years later. He soon expanded this name to *The North River Steamboat of Clermont,* which the public eventually shortened to *Clermont,* the word Fulton had added to compliment a financial backer having a Hudson River estate of that name.[4]

A unique ship called *Connector* (ca. 1858), launched in Scotland, was constructed so that individual holds could be disconnected and left in port while others were picked up, thus keeping the powerplant portion of the ship more or less continuously active. However, the connections for *Connector* proved inadequate on her maiden voyage and she sank.[5]

In some periods the type designation was added as part of the name. Many were added on seventeenth-century English warships, although it is not really clear whether such type designations were official. Among the many examples in the English men-of-war lists covering the period from 1509 to 1700 were *Dove pink, Margaret galiot, Elizabeth hoy, Eagle shallop, Mary flyboat, Mary ketch, Charles galley, Dragon sloop, Castle frigate,* and *Sheerness waterboat.*[6] Since a number of the foregoing names, and others not cited, were carried at the same time by other vessels without the type designations, perhaps type designations were added to avoid confusion. On the other hand, maybe the same vessel was entered into old records sometimes one way and sometimes the other. Although France and the United Netherlands apparently did not use type designations, occasional type designations were added to names in seventeenth-century Brandenburg, Sweden, and Denmark-Norway.[7]

Catamaran (1967) is a modern type name, carried by a twinhulled Spanish ferry. *Lloyd's* also listed *Brigantine* for a motor vessel; this usage like that of *clipper* and *frigate* in modern compound names does not indicate actual types but rather suggests speed or the romantic past.

In contrast to ships' being named for a type, many naval classes have been named after the first ship of a particular kind. In several instances ship names even became generic terms widely used by the general population. This happened with *Monitor* (1862), describing similar floating ironclad batteries. It also happened when the very old name *Dreadnought* chanced to be applied to a new kind of heavily armed battleship, and for over fifty years it was a term for any battleship.

35. Function or Cargo

Allied to type names are those ship names designating or suggesting function or cargo.

Consider *Flip*, a modern example. This long, tubular craft was designed to be towed to successive stations horizontally and then flipped vertically by flooding ballast tanks, thus becoming a stable platform in deep Pacific waters for oceanographic scientists. Like the name of a similar craft, *Pop*, for *P*erpendicular *O*cean *P*latform, *Flip* is an acronym, for *Fl*oating *I*nstrument *P*latform, although it is uncertain which came first, the descriptive name or the acronym.[1] Another example of a functional name was *Deepsea Miner* for a vessel designed to drop a gigantic vacuum tube 3,000 feet to the Atlantic floor to suck up manganese nodules or other material.[2]

An earlier example was *Scourge*, which aptly described the function of the New York privateer that took twenty-five British prizes during the War of 1812.[3] From a still earlier period, the name *Bramble* (1656) admirably suited the function of that seventeenth-century Royal Navy guard ship that was supposed to be as prickly to pass by as the name implied.[4]

Turtle (1775) well described the first craft that actually navigated under water, David Bushnell's one-man submarine.[5] Other names referring to function included *Floating Engine* (1800) and *Christmas Seal* (1943). The former, a scow propelled by twelve oarsmen, was New York City's first fireboat.[6] The city subsequently had one called *Smoke* and another called *Fire Fighter*. *Christmas Seal*, operated out of Saint John's by the Newfoundland Tuberculosis Association, was named for the special stamps sold each year to finance the boat's medical mission.[7]

Ship names designating both function and cargo included the fast ships that carried mail or news dispatches and sometimes advertised this fact in their names. *Mail* frequently was incorporated in the name of the ship. The clippers *Ocean Telegraph* (1851), *Carrier Pigeon* (1852), and *Reporter* (1853) had names indicating news carriers.[8] To scoop competitors the New York newspaper *Journal of Commerce* in 1828 sent schooners far out to sea to meet incoming vessels bearing news of particular interest to bankers and merchants. Its first schooner had the same name as the newspaper; a second was called *Evening Edition*.[9]

In the records names designating ship cargo were commoner than those indicating function. Between 1789 and 1867 four trading vessels called *Hardware* were registered at the port of New York.[10] *Codfish* was a Boston schooner of about 1790 engaged in exporting dried or salted cod.[11] Six years later *Otter* out of Boston, the first American vessel to anchor in California waters, was collecting sea otter pelts for the Canton trade.[12] In 1877 the Tudor Ice Company of Boston launched *Iceberg* and *Ice King* to carry ice to the Indies, but after the novelty of ice in the tropics wore off, the ships were mostly used for general cargo.[13] Names suggestive of cargo were given by the Sewalls of Bath, Maine, to four ships built for the California grain trade. These were *Granger* (1873), *Harvester* (1875), *Reaper* (1876) and *Thrasher* (1876). Other shipowners got into the grain-trade nomenclature with *Sower* (ca. 1875) and *Gatherer* (1874).[14]

Among cargo names for ships today in *Lloyd's* were *Louisiana Sulphur* (1943) and *Louisiana Brimstone* (1965), two sulfur carriers. *Sugar Exporter* (1960) of London was engaged in the sugar trade, as were the *crystal* ships of Sugar Line of London, including *Crystal Cube* (1955). A Montreal cement company could not have been more explicit when it called its vessel *Cementkarrier* (1930). *Deep Freeze* (1958) was a Liberian refrigeration freighter and *Japan Carryall* (1971) a Tokyo container ship. (The latter recalls the Philadelphia brig *Carry All* of about 1826.)[15] A fleet of liquid-gas carriers operated by Methane Tankers included *Methane Princess* (1964) and *Methane Progress* (1964), while an Oslo liquified-gas tanker was called *Gas Master* (1969). *Long Lines* (1961) described a 511-foot American ship capable of carrying 2,300 miles of continuous telephone cable for laying beneath the sea.[16]

36. Paired Names

Besides designating cargo, the names of the aforementioned sugar and methane ships are also good examples of series naming, an extension of paired naming, which will be examined first. Paired names are those that appropriately go together because of associations, for example, from history, religion, science, literature, legend, or linguistics.

Frobisher on his 1578 voyage seeking the Northwest Passage sailed in *Gabriel* accompanied by *Michael*, both recalling archangels.[1] John Davis, also seeking that passage in 1585, took two barks called, in the spelling of Hakluyt, *Sunneshine* and *Mooneshine*. The *Ark*, with her pinnace appropriately called *Dove*, landed colonists in Maryland in 1634.[2] Discovery of the Northeast Passage from the western side of the American continent was one objective in 1741 of Vitus Bering in *Saint Peter* and Alexai Tchirikoff in *Saint Paul*; Tchirikoff first sighted North America by sailing east and survived Bering to fill in roughly that vast vacant space then existing on world charts and extending from Alexander Archipelago to Attu Island.[3] A few years earlier *Duke* and *Duchess*, privateers, were sent out from Bristol by English merchants to prey on Spanish shipping.[4] A few years later, in 1790, two French vessels, *Compass* (*Boussole*) and *Astrolabe*, made scientific observations on the American western coast.[5] In the 1850s two Aberdeen-built Scottish tea ships complemented one another as *Robin Hood* and *Friar Tuck*.[6]

In modern times, the famous steamers *Yale* (1907) and *Harvard* (1907), decorated with colors and motifs suggesting the universities, ran between Boston and New York for several years. After time out during World War I as English Channel transports, they coasted between San Francisco and San Diego or Los Angeles until *Harvard* was wrecked in 1931 and *Yale* laid up in 1935.[7] Another pair of western steamers consisted of *Great Northern* (1914) and *Northern Pacific* (1915). Although planned as part of a transportation system by James J. Hill, head of the railroads bearing those names, they went to sea as transports in World War I. *Great Northern* between the wars became *H. F. Alexander*, and in World War II was the transport *George S. Simonds*.[8] As another example of paired passenger liners there were the "splendid sisters," *Southern Cross* (1955) and *Northern Star* (1962), the Shaw Savill round-the-world vessels.[9] The Seven Brothers Shipping Corporation of Manila had freighters called *Seven Generals* (1941) and *Seven Kings* (1945), which are consanguinity names of an unusual sort.[10]

37. Series Names

A natural extension of doublets are names all beginning with the same letter or the same syllable; or ending with the same letter or syllable; or containing a common key word; or denoting one class of ideas, persons, places, or things; or constituting a combination of the foregoing.

When series names are used, however, they are not always arbitrarily applied to all ships of a line. Changed conditions may make continued use of the series pattern unsuitable. The nomenclature may also vary with vessel type and size. On the other hand, appropriate series naming obviously is helpful as a memory device in the internal operation of a large shipping business (although it may merely satisfy some administrator's sense of order). By identifying ships under one ownership, name patterns have advertising value. They may aggrandize a family. They may have sentimental or economic overtones. And they may be intended to flatter a government or racial group with which the line intends to do business.

As one early example of series naming, *Great Sun*, *Full Moon*, and *Morning Star* were among the six ships of that doughty Dutchman Joris Spillenberg, who in 1815 smashed a Spanish fleet in the South Pacific.[1] During the last 100 to 200 years, among navies of the world, the Royal Navy stands out for the variety of its series names (more properly, class names). These class names ranged through geography, weaponry, mythology, sports, and dance; they covered birds, other animals, and flowers; they included key letters, syllables, and words; they have even had *Boxer*, *Blazer*, and *Bruiser* for hounds in a first lord's hunting pack.

Two early American examples of series naming would be the *Washington* ships of John Brown, Providence, Rhode Island, who in 1780 had *George Washington*, *General Washington*, and *President Washington*,[2] and the *continent* ships of Joseph T. Wood, Wiscasset, Maine, who had *Africa* (1810), *America* (ca. 1809), *Asia* (1810), and *Europe* (1811).[3] Another early American instance of series naming was that by the Boston and Liverpool Packet Company, organized in 1821, which had four square-rigged ships called *Amethyst*, *Emerald* (1822), *Sapphire* (1825), and *Topaz* (1822).[4] The last had a tragic ending in 1830 while en route from Calcutta to Boston; pirates murdered everybody aboard and sank the ship. Ships built at Bath, Maine, by the Houghtons all received geographical names ending in *ia*, including *Austria* (1869), *Armenia* (1877), *Persia* (1860), *Scotia* (1865), and *Samaria* (1876).[5]

Because Ferdinand Laeisz had a curly-headed daughter-in-law he called by a pet name, he assigned that name, *Poodle* (*Pudel*, 1856), to a three-masted bark, first in a long series of Laeisz ships all with *P* names. *Preussen* (1902), only five-masted full-rigged ship ever to sail the seas, along with *Pamir* and *Parma*, among others, about two dozen in all, became popularly known in English as the "Flying P Line."[6]

Sir William Garthwaite, another owner of windjammers, some remaining in service until 1929, incorporated part of his own name in *Garthpool* (1891), *Garthwray* (1889), and in a number of others.[7]

If my memory is not mistaken, the Cunard Line had an even 100 ships with names ending in *ia*, such as *Carpathia* (1903), *Berengaria* (1912), and *Saxonia* (1964). It is untrue that *Queen Mary* (1934) was the first to break the pattern; in the midnineteenth century there were seven interruptions. The usual story told about *Queen Mary* is that she was to have been christened *Victoria*, but when the Cunard chairman approached King George V to ascertain whether there would be any objection to naming a liner after a queen of England, the King replied that Queen Mary would be pleased to permit the use of her name, and that scuttled *Victoria*. However, that story has been branded as pure myth.[8] Because of the merger of Cunard, which used *ia* endings on ship names, with Oceanic, which used *ic* endings, a break with tradition was indicated, and secretly and provisionally the name *Queen Mary* was chosen, since the Queen herself had agreed to officiate at the launching. Unfortunately, two other British ships carried the chosen name. A Commonwealth country that owned one agreed to a name change, but the other *Queen Mary* was operated by Williamson Buchanan Steamers, carrying passengers on the Clyde, and the name was an asset. After extended negotiations this company agreed to call the river steamer *Queen Mary II*. Next, approval for using the name was obtained from the King. But still the chosen name was kept a close secret, the construction designation of "Number 534" being retained until the Queen herself spoke the name on launching day. Not even John Masefield, who as poet laureate wrote a poem for the occasion, was informed, with the result that his contribution appeared under the title "Number 534." The truth of the *Queen Mary* name selection may lie somewhere between the "myth" and the "true" story.

During the reign of the earlier queen, *Victoria* (1872) was a vessel in the Anchor Line series, most of which, beginning with *Alexandria*

(1870), ended in *ia*. The Allan Line and the Leyland Line both used names ending in *ian*.[9]

The Inman Line had twenty-five *city* ships, ranging from *City of Antwerp* (1867) to *City of Washington* (1853); the Castle Line had thirty-two *castle* ships, from *Arundel Castle* (1894) to *Windsor Castle* (1873); and the Nelson Line had seventeen *highland* vessels, from *Highland Brae* (1910) to *Highland Warrior* (1911).[10]

The present-day, large-scale use of series names is indicated by page after page in *Lloyd's* and *Lloyd's List of Shipowners*. Central Gulf Steamship Corporation of New Orleans had *Green Bay* (1945) to *Green Valley* (1945), the Isthmian Lines of New York had twenty-four ships from *Steel Admiral* (1944) to *Steel Worker* (1945), and William Thompson and Company of Edinburgh had *Benarty* (1963) to *Benwyvis* (1966). William Robertson of Glasgow used gem names *Amber* (1956) to *Tourmaline* (1962). Rederi A/B Transatlantic of Sweden assigned cloud names, *Nimbus* (1947), *Stratus* (1948), and *Cumulus* (1950). Maritime Fruit Carriers of Haifa have *Avocadocore* (1965), *Bananacore* (1965), and *Lemoncore* (1964). The *fern* series of A/S Glittre, Oslo, included over twenty names from *Fernbank* (1955) to *Fernwood* (1957). Sweet Lines of Manila had thirteen inter-island vessels running from *Sweet Bless* to *Sweet Trip*.

Other series names include the mythological series of the Blue Funnel Line, the bird series of General Steam Navigation Company, and the *President* series of American President Line, the *Clan* series numbering nineteen of the Clan Line steamers, the *Hawaiian* series of fifteen of Matson Steamship Line, and the *Vishva* series numbering forty of the Shipping Corporation of India.

With the advent of the great tanker fleets, series naming reached its peak and thereafter went into an apparent decline, perhaps in part because of the widespread practice of chartering. For some of his tankers Stavros Niarchos used the *World* prefix (*World Gallantry*, 1957), and his rival, Aristotle Onassis, used *Olympic* (*Olympic Fame*, 1965). Altogether there were seventy-one ships in *Lloyd's* with a *World* prefix and fifty-four with *Olympic*, but how many were controlled by the individuals named is uncertain. Public anger over oil spills may influence some petroleum firms to use names in the future not identified with their retail operations. But renaming is unlikely for the existing tanker fleets of such major concerns as British Petroleum with its *British* fleet of seventy-three or more, the *Texaco* fleet of approximately one-hundred, and the fleet of about two-hundred *Esso* ships (now *Exxon* ships for those in American waters).

According to a pilot who guided many Shell tankers into the port of Los Angeles, each ship had somewhere aboard, suitably mounted and displayed, a specimen of the shell that supplied the name. In at least two of the company's ships, however—or so he was told—the shells were so rare and valuable that replicas were displayed, while the originals reposed in the ships' safes. The use of shell names by the Royal Dutch Shell organization began before the turn of the century with *Murex* (1892) and her sister ships including *Conch* (1892) and *Volute* (1893).[11] However, this naming series apparently has been abandoned.

38. Safe Return

Another class of names expresses the age-old hope for safety at sea. This hope, to be sure, is implicit in the naming of ships after divinities and saints. But there is also a more specific type of nomenclature, such as *Speedy Return*.[1] The period of James I saw *Blessing of God*, *Due Return*, *God Save Her, Good Hope*, and *Help at Need*.[2] Sometimes a personal name was combined with a wish for good fortune, as in *Elizabeth Bonaventure* (1581), which sailed in 1585 with Drake (who also had *Hope*), or earlier as in *Edward Bonaventure*, a Sebastian Cabot ship, along with *Bona Esperanza* and *Bona Confidentia*.[3] Other often used English names in this category include *Hopewell*, *Speedwell*, and *Swiftsure*.[4]

Many modern names likewise express direct or implied hope for safety at sea. One such was *Guardian Carrier* (1957), small New Zealand freighter; another, *Safe Philippine Anchorage* (1943).[5]

One of the oldest of maritime superstitions, probably predating Roman times and surviving until the last of the windjammers, involved the nailing of a shark's fin or tail to the bow or the bowsprit. Although the exact meaning of this custom has not survived, in general it indicated the hope for a safe passage and prompt return. Perhaps originally it had something to do with a shark deity leading fishermen to a good catch. That the superstition did not die out but only changed was evident from the name of a Los Angeles fishing boat, *Sharkfin* (1943), probably chosen when hunting sharks for their vitamin-rich livers was still profitable.[6]

39. Exploration and Science

No name has been more favored by explorers than *Discovery*, a name with origins in the last half of the sixteenth century. Doubtless in the beginning it seemed an apt choice for a ship intended for exploration. Later it acquired historical significance. Perhaps its continuing popularity discloses a surviving half conscious reliance upon early name magic, in which the name was thought to influence the accomplishment. Between 1601 and 1615 George Weymouth, Henry Hudson, Thomas Button, and Robert Bylot with William Baffin all sailed in, or were accompanied by, a *Discovery* on voyages of Arctic exploration. Apparently in each case it was the same vessel, a pinnace of about twenty tons, that also sailed to Virginia in 1606 with *Susan Constant* (or *Sarah Constant*) and *Godspeed*, Captain John Smith being in the party.[1]

But the list does not end there. James Cook on his third voyage in 1776–80 had *Discovery* and *Resolution* (names identical with those of Button's vessels in 1612); and a young seaman aboard *Discovery*, George Vancouver, who at the age of fourteen had served aboard *Resolution* on Cook's previous voyage, later gained fame himself as an explorer and commanded a new *Discovery*.[2] The Russian czar in 1819 sent the corvette *Discovery* (*Otkryitie*), together with *Well-Intentioned* (*Blagonamyorenny*) on yet another search for a northern passage.[3] Captain H. F. Stephenson, second in command of a British expedition that partly traced the coasts of Ellesmere Island and Greenland, put another *Discovery* into Discovery Harbor in August of 1875.[4] A quarter of a century later Robert Scott sailed for Antarctica with yet another *Discovery*, launched in 1901 and powered by sail and steam.[5] Mount Discovery and Discovery Inlet are on Antarctica charts. *Discovery* (1962) was also a research ship of the British National Institute of Oceanography.[6] Doubtless the name will survive well into the future.

About the time Vancouver was exploring the northwestern Pacific, two Spanish naval corvettes were in the same area on a scientific expedition that surveyed much of California and finally circled the world (1789–94). One of these corvettes was called *Discovered* (officially, *Santa Justa*) by the expedition leader, Alejandro Malaspina, but more frequently he referred to her as the feminine *Discoverer* (*Descubridora*).[7]

Another ship name perpetuated for centuries was *Gabriel*, after the archangel of the Annunciation. Perhaps that choice reflected the fervent hope of explorers to announce the location of new lands. When Vasco da Gama rounded Africa for India in 1497–99, *Saint Gabriel* was his flagship.[8] Martin Frobisher sailed in *Gabriel* to the icy bay that bears his name.[9] Vitus Bering and Alexai Tchirikoff, during their first expedition in 1728, sailed *Saint Gabriel* far past Bering Strait to determine that Asia and North America were not connected, as many believed.[10]

The world's first major oceanographic vessel, the steam corvette *Chal-*

lenger (1858), bearing a name already old among English ship names, made history with Darwin aboard. Her name will probably be carried on by other oceanographic successors, such as *Glomar Challenger* (1968), the first deep-sea drilling vessel for research, operated by Glomar Marine.

Nautilus launched by Robert Fulton in 1800 was another craft that produced a string of namesakes. This twenty-one-foot, three-man, hand-powered submarine functioned satisfactorily in quiet French waters.[11] In 1958 the United States nuclear submarine *Nautilus* (1954) went to the North Pole under the ice and charted a course that cut 5,000 miles off the sea distance between Europe and Japan. The navy had several earlier surface craft and a 1909 submarine of the same name.

40. Unusual Names

In all ship records, old and recent, many names impress one as being unusual or odd, if not downright objectionable. Usually, but not always, such names belong to privately owned ships where the whim of an individual has free play. Many seem strange only because we live in a different age; others seem unusual for any age.

Sometimes names seem strange because meanings change. As an example, *Minion* (1523), for a twenty-two-ton pleasure boat, in French meant "dainty" or "darling" and in English "favorite" or "mistress," whereas today the name suggests a servile dependent.[1] A minion was also a type of ancient naval gun, a smaller type culverin, as were the saker and falcon. Both *Saker* and *Falcon* were built in 1545 at the end of the reign of Henry VIII.[2] It was Henry who not only encouraged English gun founders to rival the Flemish masters, but also introduced brass or bronze muzzle-loading guns to set the pattern for more than 200 years. It is no more than possible that the aforementioned vessels were armed with light cannon having matching names.

One name in the Anderson list of early English warships is especially intriguing, that of the twenty-ton *Falcon in the Fetterlock* (1546). A fetterlock was a device attached to the foot of a horse to prevent its running away; it consisted of a cylinder with a chain attached in the form of a D, one end fixed and the other secured by a lock. An unlikely thing to name a ship after, until it is realized that the fetterlock was also a heraldic device and was sometimes figured on a brooch. Thus the name referred to a crest showing a falcon within a fetterlock D.

Ship names may also appear odd because of obsolete spelling. In the case of *Roo* (1545), an eighty-ton English ship, of several possible meanings, the probable one is roe.³ *Squynkyn* (1322) is meaningless today but very likely came from *swinken*, a form of *swink*, meaning to gain by labor.⁴ *Pickle*, a Royal Navy schooner during the Napoleonic period, had the Scottish meaning of *little*.

Some meanings are unclear because of our unfamiliarity with life in former times. The ship name *Sweepstake* (1535) had nothing to do with a horserace but signified willingness to gamble the whole stake on a sea-fight with shares to the victor.⁵

Printing, common education, radio, and television have successively done much to erase dialects and regionalisms. *Dumble* and *Loblollypot* sailed in the days of James I.⁶ The first name is a variant of *dimble*, meaning a dingle or ravine with a watercourse. The second name, odd at any time, meant a gruel or soup pot.

A rather unusual name, often denoting fireships, was *Salamander*, with a history, both in the British Isles and on the Continent, dating from the sixteenth century. Although referring to a small lizardlike creature or a spirit supposed to live in fire, as a ship name it could have derived more directly from the heated iron used aboard for firing guns. However, the first of the Royal Navy *Salamander* ships, a 300-ton Scottish prize of 1544, previously a French vessel, very likely was named to honor Francis I of France, whose personal device was a Salamander.⁷ A London merchant *Salamander* fought against the Armada. The Dutch had four ships of that name, one a 1672 fireship; Brandenburg had three, one a 1679 fireship; and the French had a 1693 light frigate and a 1696 bomb vessel.⁸ Today West Germany has a *Salamander* landing craft.⁹

The names that follow constitute a mixed bag of oddities. *Jew's Harp* (as translated from the Dutch) in 1674 brought news to New York that Holland had ceded the colony to England.¹⁰ Perhaps the sound of wind through the rigging suggested the name. An English fireship of about 1652 was called *Mousenest*.¹¹ Could a mouse's nest have been useful tinder for catching a spark from flint and steel in firemaking? Another puzzler is why a steamship operated on the Hudson about 1817 by Thomas Gibbons was called *Mouse of the Mountain*.¹² *Who's Afraid* was a British privateer of 1780 and *Sturdy Beggar* an American privateer out of Salem, Massachusetts, of the same period.¹³ For some obscure reason another Salem privateer of about 1812 was named *Grumbler and Growler*.¹⁴ *Merry Quaker* of Bristol, Massachusetts, seemed far from merry to the slaves she carried from Africa to Havana; there she was sold in 1795 because it was too expensive to clean out the filth from the slave cargo.¹⁵ *Precious Ridicule* was a New Orleans schooner built in 1806 and *Free Love* a Mississippi barge enrolled in 1817.¹⁶ *Free Love*, however, might have been intended for the feminine name *Freelove,* which, like certain other seventeenth- and eighteenth-century English and American names, was not limited to girls. Similar names given to either sex appeared on ships, such as *Comfort, Deliverance, Experience, Increase, Peace,* and *Temperance.* The challenge inherent in *Catch Me Who Can* (or *Catch Me If You Can*), letter-of-marque schooner from Baltimore, may have spurred on H.M.S. *Colibri* to do just that in 1812 off Cape Sable.[17] One wonders what happened on *The Twenty-Sixth Day of October 1812,* for that was the name of a British schooner captured in 1814 by an American privateer.[18] Was it the launch date, a birth date, a marriage date? Perhaps the date a previous vessel was lost, a loss the new vessel was to avenge? The name of *Gallinipper* (1823), an American row-barge stationed at the West Indies naval station, was composed of *galley* and the colloquial term *nipper* for a large mosquito or other stinging insect.[19] A policeboat built in 1894 at Cambridge, Maryland, sailed as *Brown Smith Jones.*[20] This name apparently was compounded of the names of three Maryland state officials. One of the first steamboats on Lake Erie, *Walk-on-the-Water,* derived her name from an old Indian's description of Fulton's *Clermont* paddling up the Hudson.[21] That a primitive mind should so characterize a craft with side paddles rotating like strange feet is consistent with the very essence of naming as seen in some Babylonian names.

Some unusual names reflected economic realities, perhaps nostalgia for the land. The name of the seventeenth-century English ship *Poor Man's Plough* may have expressed land hunger, not uncommon when younger sons, scarcely hoping to own land, followed a life at sea less by choice than by necessity.[22] Possibly *Flying Cow* from the same period likewise expressed a rural longing, as perhaps did *Cherry Tree* and maybe *Black Bess,* which could be a horse's name (if not that of a mistress).[23] Another example with a rural flavor was *Ploughboy,* a New Orleans privateer of about 1812.[24] Two early nineteenth-century Maine vessels were *Pyed Cow* and *Farmer's Fancy,* the latter, although only 126 tons, a full-rigged ship.[25] *Blade of Wheat* (1689) sounds agrarian; it may have expressed the hope of profitable increase from the biblical verse as rendered in the King James version, "first the blade, then the ear, after that the full corn in the ear."[26]

Casket would appear to be an unlikely ship name, especially now when it carries the meaning of coffin; however, two brigs and a schooner out of New York had this name between 1815 and 1837.[27] At approximately the same time *Cabinet* was entered at New Orleans.[28] Possibly both these names were inspired by a clergyman's having cited the literal Hebrew

meaning of *ark* as being casket or chest. Many craft throughout history
have been named *Ark*, including five listed in *MVUS68*.

Sometimes circumstances of design or construction produce out-of-the
ordinary names, such as *Trial*, a Royal Navy cutter of about 1790, which
had multiple drop keels;[29] *First Effort* (1830), William Collyer's first
design, a Hudson River sloop;[30] and *Surprise*, a Massachusetts clipper
launched fully rigged in 1850.[31]

The ship (later bark) *Top Gallant* (1863), built in East Boston and
finally dropped from registry in 1900, may have been the only vessel ever
named for a sail, although a rare usage of that term meant summit or
zenith, obviously deriving from the sail's high position.[32]

In the days of sail Canada had a sixty-ton Newfoundland schooner
called *Go-ask-her* (1855), a smaller Yarmouth schooner *Essence of Pep-
permint* (1877), and a full-rigged ship built at Saint John's for the East
India trade and named *Beejapore* (1851) after the cannon said to have
been the largest in the world when captured by the British from the
Sikhs.[33]

Cricket was the odd name of a Union admiral's flagship, a "tin-clad
steamboat" used in the Red River campaign of 1864.[34] One would probably not be far from the mark in suspecting this wooden paddlewheeler
sounded like a gigantic cricket, indeed, when her "tin" panels crinkled
under stress or "oil-canned" when heated by the sun and then contracted
again at night. Another Civil War oddity, *Intelligent Whale*, a thirty-
foot hand-cranked submarine that six to thirteen men could operate
under water for several hours, is preserved in the Washington Navy
Yard.

In *Yachting* magazine an article on "Inconsistencies in Vessels'
Names," dealt with vessels, mostly schooners, trading out of Atlantic
Coast ports of the United States sometime before the turn of the century.
Tarry Not (probably 1870, Addison, Maine) once sailed from Maine for
Philadelphia in November with a cargo of Christmas trees and didn't
arrive until Washington's Birthday. *Big Bonanza* (probably 1875, New-
buryport, Massachusetts, a Down Easter) was sold for debt four times
in thirteen years. *Only Son* (perhaps 1856, brig of Biddeford, Maine)
was owned and commanded by a man who had seven brothers and four
sons. Among others mentioned in the article, *Hard Luck* was unusually
lucky on the fishing banks; the bark *Brilliant Sailor* held a record for the
longest time crossing the Atlantic, and *Prohibition* had a captain who
seldom went to sea sober. *Snowflake* was painted green, *White Cloud*
black, and *Black Bird* red.[35]

Several names mentioned previously certainly do little credit to ship
or owner. But none were so bad as *Rotten Apple* and *Horse Turd*, which

sailed English waters in the days of James I.[36] It is possible these were forthright protests by dissatisfied purchasers. While there are unworthy names today, as reference to registers shows, there may be none to compare with those two of the early seventeenth century.

41. Contemporary Influences

Contemporary events are reflected in many ship names. Events significant in a nation's life may produce names that are religious, political, or warlike in nature. However, many contemporary influences are inconsequential, being fads, dances, songs, slang, scientific innovations, or whatever happens to capture the interest of a few persons or the imaginations of many. Most contemporary names appear briefly and then disappear. However, some are carried on, although the original significance of the name may be obscured or even lost. For instance, the literal Hebrew meaning "Yahweh is gracious" for *John* is rarely if ever considered when naming a child; rather John is chosen because it sounds well or has been used in the family.

Today names with a contemporary flavor are most likely to appear on pleasure craft, for which the average term of ownership is probably less than five years, each new owner being likely to select a new name. I speculated about the name *The Lady in Cement* across the transom of a large power cruiser and finally asked; it was the title of a motion picture. *Kentucky Colonel*, another power cruiser, referred not to the honorary title bestowed by the governor of an American state but to a food franchising chain.

However, such names are by no means limited to pleasure craft. According to *Lloyd's*, both a French fishing boat (1963) and a Liberian tanker (1943) had the name of a cartoon character, *Popeye*. A Panamanian freighter carried the name of a television program, *Star Trek* (1944). *Lloyd's* also listed *Telstar* thrice, for French, Dutch, and Belgian ships, as well as *Sputnik* (1958) for a Russian one. Both *Flying Saucer* and *Astronaut* were fairly common names on commercial craft, according to *MVUS68*, while in *Lloyd's* was a United States Lines freighter called *American Astronaut* (1969). Perhaps before long we shall see *Ecological Concern* on a petroleum supertanker.

In 1925 the naming of a new saint caused a number of fishing craft to be called *Saint Therese* or *Little Flower*, her sobriquet. Robert Louis Stevenson was known as Tusitala, "Teller of Tales," in the South Seas community where he spent his last years. One of the last full-rigged American flag ships, Scottish built, carried the name *Tusitala* (1883)

into the early 1930s. She operated year-round from New York to Honolulu carrying fertilizer, sometimes returning to Baltimore with sugar, or
going to Puget Sound with Waikiki sand ballast and then to Baltimore
with lumber.[1] A seaman who served aboard told me that a bronze plate
on the mainmast explained the origin of the name. In connection with
the celebration of 100 years of nationhood in 1876, several dozen American vessels built in that year carried the name *Centennial*.

Shangri-La appeared sixteen times in *MVUS68*. In the years before
World War II this imaginary land, described in the novel *Lost Horizons*,
appeared as the name of only three registered United States vessels. Then
early in the war President Roosevelt jokingly made Shangri-La famous
by announcing it as the secret place from which B-25 light bombers took
off for the first bombing of Tokyo. The year 1944 saw the launching of
a United States carrier called *Shangri-La*.

Teddy Bear was a two-masted schooner trading along the Arctic coast
about 1910.[2] Earlier in the century Theodore "Teddy" Roosevelt, in a
much-publicized incident, refused while hunting to shoot a bear cub, and
this publicity produced the name "Teddy Bear," a name soon applied to
the stuffed plaything beloved by millions of children. The clipper ship
Nightingale (1851) shows that names are not always what they seem.[3]
Built at Portsmouth, New Hampshire, the clipper was not named for a
bird at all, at least not directly, but for Jenny Lind, the "Swedish Nightingale." After use in the China trade *Nightingale* was a slaver until captured in 1861 and taken into the United States Navy.

The bark *Fluorine* (1881), built to haul cryolite ore (aluminum fluor-
ide) from Greenland to the United States, hit the water at Bath, Maine,
at the time when the world was keenly interested in efforts (soon to be
successful) to isolate the new element fluorine which Ampere had
named in 1814.[4]

Soon after men first took to the sky in balloons, *Aeronaut* (1837) ap-
peared on a whaler out of New London, Connecticut.[5] The fabulous
Crystal Palace of glass and iron was still a wonder in London when
Crystal Palace (1864) slid into the water at Eastport, Maine.[6] Crystal
Palace was also a nineteenth-century amusement center with caged ani-
mals in lower New York City. Although the last traces of the Crystal
Palace in England disappeared in 1941, the name persists, as do many
names after being introduced. In 1971 I saw the name on a power cruiser.

Whoever named *Bull, Bear, and Horse*, an English ship of the first
quarter of the seventeenth century, must have been a devotee of the sport
of baiting those animals, that is, by setting dogs to attack a bull or bear
chained to a stake or a pony running madly with a monkey strapped to
its back.[7]

CHAPTER VII

Name Forms

42. The Definite Article

PROPERLY a part of Spanish and some other foreign ship names mentioned herein, the definite article has been dropped to conform to our usage. At one time the definite article was an inseparable part of French ship names; with German and Scandinavian ships its use appears to have been arbitrary.

Without going further into the history of this usage, it is perhaps sufficient to note the occurrence of the definite article in two present-day registers. *MVUS68* had entries as follows: *The* (306 total, but only 11 for vessels of over 1,000 gross tons), *El* (120), *Los* (8), *La* (113), *Las* (0), *L'* (0), *Le* (16), and *Der* (3). These entries totaled 566, just over 0.8 percent of the entries. *Lloyd's* had entries as follows: *The* (13), *El* (68), *Los* (6), *La* (88), *Las* (10), *L'* (8), *Le* (41), and *Al* (56). These totaled 290, or about 0.6 percent of entries. The *Lloyd's* total would be considerably higher if Scandinavian words incorporating the definite article were included. The article appears in the ending of Swedish ship names as *en* in the singular and *es* in the plural or merely as *n* or *s*.

One name stands out as unusual in both registers: *The Cabins* (1959), Wilmington, Delaware, operated by The Cabins Tanker.

In *Lloyd's* were *The Lady Grania* (1952), *The Lady Gwendolen* (1953), and *The Lady Patricia* (1962), owned by Arthur Guinness Son and Company, Liverpool. These ships were apparently named for several members of the titled Guinness family, the definite article being carried over from its proper social use when writing the names of women closely related to certain peers. An appropriate use of the definite article involved the yacht built in 1931 and used occasionally by five United States presidents; when finally sold in 1970 she was suitably renamed *The Presidents*.

The United States Navy list for late 1970 had one definite article name, *The Sullivans*, a destroyer launched in 1943, one year after four sailor brothers named Sullivan were killed in action.

There were two definite articles in *The Fulton the First*, the name of the paddlewheel warship built 1814–15 for the United States Navy by Robert Fulton.[1]

A ship famous for its speed under any weather condition was *The Tweed*. Launched in India as *Punjab* (1854) and originally a paddlewheel frigate, she was acquired by John Willis in 1863, converted to sail, and renamed. Despite owning *Cutty Sark* and other vessels, Willis always considered *The Tweed* to be the flagship of his fleet. Joseph Conrad thought the fortuitous placement of the masts accounted for her excellent sailing qualities.[2]

43. Alphabetic Frequency

It may be of slight interest to note, taking *MVUS68* as evidence, that apparently more ship names in English begin with *M* than with any other letter. Almost an equal number—perhaps a larger number if other sources were consulted—begin with *S*. These are followed, not too closely, in descending order by *C, A, B, L, T, P, J, D, R, E,* and *G.* Frequency of the remaining thirteen letters drops off sharply.

44. Adjective Names

The use of adjectives to do the work of nouns is a very old practice in ship naming. Among Greek galley names were such adjectives as *Audacious, Charming,* and *Famous.* Yet despite their long history in English ship nomenclature, adjectival names often sound strange (as do occasional verbal or adverbial names), although such famous names as *Illustrious* and *Victorious,* carried by British warships and widely copied on small craft, are readily acceptable to the ear.

Perhaps the first instance in English of an adjectival name was *Nonpareil,* the designation given in 1584 to the rebuilt *Philip and Mary.*[1] *Pliant* appeared in a list of ships of the reign of James I (1605-25).[2] Sir John Hawkins's small privateer *Dainty* (also a noun) in 1592 helped capture the rich treasure of *Madre de Dios.*[3] But in those days adjective names in English were exceptional.

According to R. C. Anderson, the capture of French prizes was the principal reason for the introduction of adjectival ship names into England.[4] Among the early ship lists he examined, Pepy's list had one example, for the horseboat *Prosperous;* the Sergison list of 1702 had only *Content,* a French prize of 1685, and an English fireship *Terrible* (1694); Schomberg's list of 1727 included *Superb,* a prize, and *Happy,* a sloop, and his 1741 list retained only *Superb;* and Schomberg's 1748 list included two more prizes, *Invincible* and *Intrepid.* After that date such adjectival names became more common. At Beachy Head nearly two-thirds of the ships in the French line had adjectival names.

In Russia, also, as early as 1727, adjectives frequently were used on frigates and other small types, Anderson observed, and Spain had *Gloriosa* and *Arrogante* during the Seven Years' War and *Constante* and *Fuerte* in 1737. However, the Scandinavian, Dutch, Portuguese, and Venetian ships had names derived only from proper names and substantives.

Among many fine old English adjectival names on record were *Robust* and *Lively*[5] and *Swift*.[6] Others not so old included those of the British warship *Magnificent*[7] and the schooner *Exquisite*[8] out of London about 1830. *Brilliant* (1862), an American sternwheeler, served the Union well on inland waters during the Civil War.[9] *Alert* of Boston, which brought Richard Henry Dana home from California, figured in *Two Years Before the Mast*.

Many modern vessels carry adjectival names. *Righteous* (1969) was a Liberian bulk carrier. Others in *Lloyd's* included *Brisk* (1965) of Norway; *Courageous* (1943), San Diego fisherman; *Rigorous* (1959), British tug; and *Dynamic* (1958), Liberian ore and oil carrier.

The greatest use of adjectives is in compound names. Adjectives (or words used as adjectives) frequently found as modifiers include: *American, Black* (also *Green* and *Blue*), *British, Columbia, Eastern* (along with *Northern, Southern,* and *Western*), *Empire, Flying, Golden, Grand, Great, Indian, Island, Little, New, Sea, Silver,* and *Young*. Such usage, however, does not suggest that something is missing, as adjectival and adverbial names standing alone frequently do.

Then there are the words run together, such as the very old names *Swiftsure* combining two adjectives, *Tryright* combining a verb with an adverb, as does *Hopewell*, and *Dreadnaught* combining a verb with a noun.[10] (*Swiftsure*, however, probably originated as *Swift-suer,* that is, "Swift-pursuer.")

45. Verb Names

Verb names are infrequent in ship records. I can recall seeing only two on actual vessels, *Rush* on a yacht and *Retrieve* on a harbor craft. The strictly verbal name in English—that is, the name that cannot also be considered a noun—seems usually to have been limited, for whatever obscure reason, to relatively small craft. A brief perusal of *Lloyd's* disclosed no verb names, although several probably were listed. The yield from a scanning of *MVUS68* was five definite verb names, all on yachts, fishing boats, or other small vessels.

MVUS68 listed *Excel* three times for fishing boats, *Gamble* for a

Louisiana oil-exploration vessel, *Rejoice* and *Relax* for yachts, and *Remember* for a Louisiana towboat. Names that were probably verbs included *Ply* for an Alaskan fisherman, *Rescue* for a towboat, and *Skip* for five small craft. Possibly verbal was *Venture*, carried by forty-seven small craft.

The Elizabethans who named *Desire* and *Delight* probably did not even consider whether the words were verbs or nouns. Being men of action, they probably thought of the names as expressing action or existence. They desired Spanish gold and delighted in sea fights to get it. Thus those names may be among the earliest verbal ones in English.

Young Thomas Cavendish took *Desire* around the world, accompanied part way by *Content*. Together in 1587 off Lower California they captured the Manila galleon *Santa Ana* with her rich cargo of pearls, silks, and 102 troy pounds of gold. *Desire* finally made it home to Plymouth and was the setting for a joyous banquet attended by Queen Elizabeth I.[1] *Delight* was one of the vessels on the last voyage, made in 1595, by Drake and Hawkins. Hakluyt recorded that she became leaky and was purposely sunk.

An old English naval name was *Fly*. The *Oxford Dictionary* states that very early the verb *fly* was associated with *flyboat*, meaning a fast boat. This strongly indicates that *Fly* had the verbal meaning when used for a shallop of 1648 and for three later small vessels of the same century.[2] *Fly* appropriately designated an American schooner built in 1810 to run the British blockade, but she was not quite fast enough and was captured.[3]

Doubt exists as to what part of speech were the names for *Transfer*, an American letter-of-marque schooner during the War of 1812;[4] the Bristol ship *Try* (1852);[5] the often used *Endeavour*; and *Romp* (1847), an Essex, Massachusetts, clipper schooner.[6] Probably *Romp* had the verbal meaning in racing parlance of moving rapidly or winning with ease.

Most certainly verbal was the name for a bark launched as *Glide* (1861) for trade with Zanzibar, not the first in New England to use the name.[7] During World War II the United States loaned the minesweeper *Adopt* (1942) to Russia and never got her back.[8]

46. Noun Names

Most numerous among ship names are common nouns, as indicated by the many noun names in earlier sections. Although on ships today the adjective-noun combination, as in *American Lark* (1969), is widely employed, names consisting of nouns alone outnumber all others. Both in number and diversity they provide a truly surprising catalog of people, places, and things.

In the appended listing are names selected at random from *Lloyd's*. While some are unique for that register, others occur in multiple entries. Only one example of each class is listed; that is, only one flower name of many. *Lloyd's* was chosen as the source because it covers mostly large vessels.

Ancient city: *Jerico* (1961), French trawler
Animal: *Beaver* (1957), Liberian tanker
Army unit: *Platoon* (1965), British tug
Artist: *Michelangelo* (1965), Italian liner
Astrological sign: *Aquarius* (1969), Liberian tanker
Astronomer: *Galileo Galilei* (1964), Russian tanker
Astronomical event: *Eclipse* (1954), American tanker
Astronomical object: *Meteor* (1964), West German fish-research vessel
Athletic event: *Olympic Games* (1964), Liberian tanker
Bandit: *Jesse James* (1923), American tug
Battle: *Bull Run* (1943), American tanker
Bird: *Oriole* (1963), British tanker
Castle: *Windsor Castle* (1960), London freighter
Cloud: *Cumulus* (1963), Dutch weather ship
Constellation: *Orion* (1963), Norwegian bulk carrier
Current: *Gulf Stream* (1965), American freighter
Dog: *Spaniel* (1955), British vessel
Explorer: *Magellan* (1958), French freighter
Fairy tale: *Snow White* (1968), Liberian bulk carrier
Fish: *Goldfish* (1961), Filipino fisherman
Flag: *Pennant* (1954), Panama tanker
Flower: *Pansy* (1951), Indian dredge
Gambling game: *Baccarat* (1965), Danish vessel
Gem: *Emerald* (1968), Liberian freighter
Geographical feature: *Plateau* (1952), British tug
Historic structure: *Melrose Abbey* (1959), British ship
Homeric heroine: *Nausicaa* (1961), Liberian bulk carrier
Horse: *Percheron* (1944), American tug
Indian tribe: *Sioux* (1964), West German tanker
Inventor: *Marconi* (1947), Belgian trawler
Islands: *Cyclades* (1939), Greek merchantman
Knot: *Bowline* (1953), British dredge
Lake: *Lake Placid* (1962), Liberian bulk carrier

Legendary hero: *Sir Lancelot* (1964), British freighter
Legendary seaman: *Sinbad* (1963), Swedish tanker
Literary character: *Hamlet* (1967), Norwegian ship
Local wind: *Monsoon* (1959), Norwegian tanker
Mariner: *Captain Cook* (1966), Canadian tug
Medical herb: *Arnica* (1946), Italian vessel
Metal: *Gold* (1951), British craft
Meteorological phenomenon: *Northern Lights* (1950), Norwegian vessel
Mineral: *Onyx* (1967), Danish trawler
Microscopic life: *Plankton* (1965), London tug
Mountain: *Mount Sinai* (1944), Greek freighter
Muse: *Clio* (1965), Helsinki freighter
Musician: *Piper* (1942), Belfast tug
Nationality: *Irishman* (1967), British salvage tug
Navigational instrument: *Sextant* (1953), West German ship
Navigational star: *Sirius* (1955), Greek tanker
Navigational term: *Meridian* (1962), Russian training ship
Novelist: *Somerset Maugham* (1961), British trawler
Opera: *Traviata* (1969), Swedish bulk freighter
Park: *Yellowstone* (1945), American bulk carrier
Philosopher: *Plato* (1955), West German vessel
Physician: *Dr. Lykes* (1945), American freighter
Planet: *Saturn* (1965), Russian fish-factory ship
Poet: *Homer* (1963), Greek bulk carrier
Pope: *Pio X* (1961), Spanish trawler
Reptile: *Viper* (1943), Nigerian ship
River: *Amazon* (1948), Greek merchantman
Scientist: *Ampere* (1951), French cable ship
Sculptor: *Phidias* (1954), Dutch freighter
Sea mammal: *Sea Lion* (1969), Belgian tug
Season: *Spring* (1947), Liberian merchantman
Song: *Stardust* (1955), Danish fisherman
Spirit: *Ariel* (1961), Norwegian bulk carrier
Spy: *Mata Hari* (1943), Indonesian vessel
Television program: *Flipper* (1969), Swedish tanker
Tree: *Spruce* (1968), Japanese freighter
Volcano: *Maunaloa II* (1899), Canadian lake steamer
Warrior: *Crusader* (1957), British freighter
Weapon: *Sword* (1954), Finnish tanker
Whale: *Grampus* (1956), Galveston tug
Miscellaneous: *Cement* (1946), Yugoslavia; *Concho* (1955), United

States; *Crofter* (1951), England; *Diplomat* (1953), England; *Galaxy* (1945), U.S.; *Pioneer* (1963), Ghana; *Sand* (1944), Norway; *Snowman* (1967), Denmark; *Spray* (1962), Scotland; *Universe* (1955), Liberia; *Viking* (1966), Sweden; *Wave* (1938), United States.

47. Numerical Names

Numerical names are not much favored in English, except for barges and sometimes tugs, but are quite common in Japan where they are not unusual for persons, places, and things. Thus a Japanese child may be called by the date of his birth or even "100–100" after perfect numbers.

As applied to ships, numerical names are of two types. The first consists of a basic common name followed, for different ships, by successive numerals. The second type is a number or a date constituting the entire name.

An example of the first type is the *Toyo Maru* series. *Lloyd's* listed seventy ships bearing that name followed by a numerical designation, among which six ships had *No. 3* and five *No. 5*. There were numerous other duplications, as well as many gaps in the numerical sequence. The *Toyo Maru* ships were not all under one ownership. The *Toyota Maru* fleet, numbered from 1 through 15, is still growing; in Japanese fashion, *No. 4* and *No. 9* were excluded as being unlucky. A Liberian line operates a fleet of tankers all named *Permina Samudra*, each differentiated by a Roman numeral.

An early numerical pattern for English ships was that of the first Royal Navy class, the Whelps, built to one design in 1628, *First Whelp* through *Tenth Whelp*. These were coast guard craft about sixty-three feet in length, each with a crew of sixty, whose principal duty originally was to suppress French and Turkish privateers in home waters. Sir Thomas Button, admiral of the king's ships on the coast of Ireland, commanded *Ninth Whelp*.[1] During World War I requisitioned vessels having names already in use by the Royal Navy were numbered, such as *Hercules II, III,* and *IV*; but in World War II, in order to avoid the confusion that resulted, this practice was not followed.[2]

The Swedes in 1676 launched thirteen *bojorts* of about the same length as the Whelps and simply numbered them 1 through 13. Others were subsequently added with higher numbers, and some of the original ones were replaced. Four Swedish "mail yachts" were numbered 1 through 4. About this same time, too, Norway had *Galley No. 1* through *Galley No. 3*.[3]

The United States also has had numbered vessels. Off New Orleans in 1814 the British captured five American gunboats simply designated *No. 5, No. 23, No. 156, No. 162,* and *No. 163.*[4] It appears that 176 of these "Jefferson gunboats," of a larger number authorized, actually were launched. They were fifty-five to seventy feet in length, had a lateen rig on two masts, carried oars, and had one or two guns. Although need for such auxiliary craft had been shown at Tripoli, probably they were funded by a Congress otherwise penurious with the navy only because "pork-barrel" contracts could go to a number of inland states.[5] The United States Navy again resorted to numerical naming during World War I, when contracts were let for 112 patrol boats, all to be called *Eagle* followed by the appropriate numeral.[6]

As indicated by *MVUS68*, tug and barge operators used hundreds of numerical sequence names, such as *Crowley No. 1* or *Barge No. 1* or simply *No. 1* (but occasionally unusual names such as *Motorless* and *Motorminus*).

A name both numerical and political was *Thirty-Fifth Parallel* (1859), for a paddlewheel steamer built in Cincinnati and operated out of New Orleans until taken into service by the Confederate Army.[7] The thirty-fifth parallel was proposed as a demarkation line between "free" North and "slave" South.

Names with prefix numerals or numbers spelled out are scarce on present-day ships. In a special section in *Lloyd's* forty-one names began with a numeral; others in the text proper included *Fifty-Two Miles*, a Nassau craft. Some names in the special section indicated significant dates or national holidays, such as *1 Mai* (1950), East German fishing boat, and *14 Ramadhan* (1962), Iraq freighter. Guinea, Uruguay, and Yemen each had a ship with a date name apparently marking a change in regime. Four Russian container ships had names prefixed by *50 Let*, celebrating fifty years of Communist rule. Union Oil Company spelled out the build date for *Nineteen Twenty-Three*, a bunkering barge operating out of San Pedro.

48. Nicknames

Whatever their real names, many ships are sometimes known or better known or only known by their nicknames.

Nicknames may be serious names, even proud ones, such as "Old Ironsides" for *Constitution* (1797). That nickname obviously produced the official name, *New Ironsides*, for the Philadelphia-built ironclad warship of 1862.[1] Almost forgotten today is that the other famed frigate, *Constellation* (1797), because of her turn of speed, in earlier days was known as "Yankee Racehorse."[2]

A nickname may convey the idea of bigness, such as "Tuttilmondo" (the whole world) given by the Venetians in 1173 to a galleon considered to be of great size, the actual name having been lost.[3] Another example is "Great Harry" for *Henri Grâce á Dieu*. Closer to our day, there was the famous sternwheel towboat *Sprague* (1902), which towed a record sixty barges in 1907 and remained active for forty-five years, being known up and down the Mississippi as "Big Mama."[4] The Mississippi produced many colorful nicknames; among those bestowed by black workers were "You Be Damn" for *Danube*, "Rebel Home" for *Richmond*, "Fuss-Maker" for *Mabel Comeaux*, and "Broken Back" for *G. W. Sentell*.[5]

Appearance may suggest a nickname. The Dutch called *Sovereign of the Seas* (1637) the "Golden Devil" because of her extensive gilded decorations.[6] *Anglia* (1866), a London sidewheeler, had three stacks and was known as "Three-Fingered Jack."[7] Because *Tashmoo* (1899), Lake Erie paddlewheel excursion steamer, had much glass to protect passengers from the wind, she was known to many as "The Glass Hack."[8] "The Covered Wagon," inspired by the movie of that name, was often applied in the navy to the first United States aircraft carrier *Langley*, created in 1921 by roofing a flight deck over the collier *Jupiter*.[9]

Sailing characteristics of a vessel, whether actual or only the way she was employed, produced nicknames. On his second voyage Columbus had a second *Santa Maria*, but she was usually called "Mariagalante" for her gallant behavior at sea.[10] During World War II sailors aboard the United States carrier escort *Hoggat Bay* called her "Hokey Pokey Maru" out of pure boredom, because most of the time she just poked around slowly among the Pacific islands.[11]

Snobbishness may be involved in nicknaming; frequent passengers on the Cunard liners *Lusitania* (1907) and *Mauretania* (1907) called them "Lucy" and "Maury."[12] Perhaps snobbishness also had something to do with the Boston nickname "Cattle Only" for *Catalonia*, one of several Cunarders in service during the last two decades of the nineteenth century, bringing many immigrants in steerage from Liverpool-Queenstown to Boston.[13]

Usually, however, nicknames originated with seamen because official names were difficult to pronounce or suggested puns. The tendency to anglicize foreign-sounding words and an inclination for humor are evident, as are a rough affection and attempts to ridicule. In "Notes" in *The Mariner's Mirror*, T. D. Manning, Edgar K. Thompson, and Lord

Bridport listed many British naval nicknames.[14] Perhaps best known of these is "Billy Ruffian" or sometimes "Belleruffan" for *Bellerophon*. The repair ship *Resource* became the despair ship "Remorse." *Weston-super-Mare* became "Aggie on Horseback," a reference to Miss Agnes Weston's Sailors' Homes. In 1823 *Thetis* was chosen for an experiment in reducing the rum ration and became known as "Tea Chest."

The following list draws further upon the aforementioned "Notes":

Achilles (Chillus)

Agamemnon (Eggs and Bacon, Aggy)

Agincourt (Gin Palace)

Amphitrite ('am and Tripe)

Andromache (Andrew Mack)

Andromeda (Andro Meda)

Ariadne (Hairy Annie)

Atalanta (Hat and Lantern)

Bacchante (Black Shant)

Beaulieu (Bowly)

Belle Poule (Bell Pull)

Belliqueux (Billy Squeaks)

Calypso (Cliphooks)

Charybdis (Cherrybis)

Cyclops (Cyclebox)

Daedalus (Deadlies)

Dedaigneuse (Dead Nose)

Euryalus (New Royalist)

Foudroyant (Fore Dragon)

Genereux (Jenny Rooks)

Hermione (Hermy One)

Latona (Let Alone)

Minotaur (Minny Tar)

Niobe (Nobby)

Penelope (Pennyloap)

Polyphemus (Polly Infamous)

Psyche (Pish, Pisky, Sitch)

Queen Elizabeth (Big Lizzie)

Ramilies (Ram)

Royal Sovereign (Royal Quid or The Quid)

Royal William (Royal Billy)

Sans Pareil (Sam Perry)

Serapis (Old Sarah)

Temeraire (Trim yer 'air or Temmy)

Terpsichore (Tapsykoar)

Trafalgar (Traffy)

Venerable (Archdeacon)

Vengeance (The Lord's Own)

Ville de Milan (Wheel 'em Along)

Ville de Paris (Willy de Parry)

Many of these names simply begged for nicknames; for others the nicknames could hardly have been foreseen. Some names, once meeting the standards of a good name, are acceptable only because of tradition. Other names, it would seem, originally were chosen with no thought whatever for the seamen who would serve aboard and find them unpronounceable or meaningless.

49. Surrogate Names

Ships identification by some means other than a name, or in addition to a name, is surrogate naming. Nicknames are surrogate names if widely used in place of the official name. Symbols on the hull or sails and on standards or emblems carried superficially have all been used for identification at various times.

An unusual example of a surrogate name was the rebus symbol carried by *Tensas* (pronounced "Ten-saw," perhaps syllables from Tennessee and Arkansas), a Mississippi steamer that survived into the first decades of the twentieth century. Suspended between her stacks was a large circular sawblade bearing the painted number *10* on each side.[1]

The United States relies upon a surrogate name, which is the official number, as the primary means of identification for registered vessels and thus permits duplication of actual names. No published list exists of these official numbers in complete numerical order, although each annual edition of *MVUS* gives the official number along with the name listed alphabetically for every vessel under current registry.

In 1970 the North American Yacht Racing Union began assigning numbers to racing sailboats. These numbers must be prominently displayed on mainsail, headsail, and spinnaker to qualify for racing. Navy and coast guard officials strongly endorsed the numbering program as an aid in search-and-rescue operations. Yacht numbers formerly represented build-sequence in each class and caused much confusion. Sail numbers are distinct from the registration numbers assigned pleasure craft by individual states or the federal number assigned documented yachts.

Another type of surrogate naming is that upon which the United States Navy primarily depends. This consists of combinations of capital letters and numerals to designate the type of ship and the number within the type. For example, CVA–67 is the attack aircraft carrier *John F. Kennedy*. SSBN–659 is the nuclear-powered, fleet-ballistic-missile submarine *Will Rogers*. DDG–23 is the guided-missile destroyer *Richard E. Byrd*. As of late 1970 the official navy list of type designations totaled 118, including auxiliary and service vessels. Understandably, type designations change with time. Where large numbers and kinds of ships are involved, such nomenclature quickly communicates not only the name but also the capabilities of each vessel and expedites the assignment of vessels at every level of command. Painted large upon ships, the designations greatly facilitate visual identifications. However, the complete designation usually does not appear; one or more of the letters may be dropped; in particular, major attack vessels customarily show only their numbers, for the silhouette discloses the type before markings can be read.

In a similar manner, the United Kingdom uses hull numbers, which are termed pennant numbers, for naval vessels. Its system is simpler than that of the United States but conveys less information. One capital letter indicates type, followed by two or more numerals indicating ship within the type. In 1970 type letters totaled fifteen, including *R* for carriers, *C* for cruisers, *D* for destroyers, *F* for frigates, and *S* for submarines.

The term *pennant numbers* harks back to yet another type of surrogate name, the code signal. Using its official signal a ship can convey name and nationality to a shore station or to another ship. This may be done by flags, but the signal is normally used today as a radio call.

The first modern naval code name consisted of a single flag peculiar to the ship. When the United States created its first real navy, vessels had such flags. Signal books from the first decade of the nineteenth century show that, among the frigates, *Adams* (1799) had a simple red burgee, or pennant, and *Chesapeake* (1799) a blue one. Square flags combining colors in designs involving stripes, squares, disks, and crosses were displayed by the frigates *Congress* (1799), *Constitution* (1797), *Essex* (1799), *New York* (1800), *Philadelphia* (1799), *President* (1800), and *United States* (1797), and likewise by ships and most brigs.[2]

Burgees are also carried by some yachts and displayed by day at the truck of the main mast or, on mastless craft, at the bow staff. Yachting tradition, doubtless to differentiate it from merchant vessel practice, dictates that the burgee design include neither letters nor numerals.

An official elaborated signal system was approved in 1803 by the British Admiralty. It was developed by Sir Home Popham and improved in 1812 to cover a vocabulary of 30,000 words. Captain Frederick Marryat adapted Popham's system for the merchant service in 1817. It was soon approved by Lloyd's and spread to the United States. Earlier and later, however, there were several other American systems.[3] The system most used by clipper ships was that revised in 1854 by Henry J. Rogers of Baltimore.

The International Code of Signals used today came into use January 1, 1902, and has since been revised extensively. It resulted from years of work and international coordination by a British committee representing shipping interests, first appointed in 1887 by the Board of Trade. The present-day flag system consists of twenty-six alphabet flags, ten numeral pennants, three repeater pennants, and one code, or answering, pennant. Hoists of one letter, two letters, or three letters convey numerous coded messages. Four-letter hoists beginning with *A* convey over 11,000 geographical names, while four-letter hoists not beginning with *A* convey a ship's name. The first letter (for some countries the first two letters) of a name hoist indicates the ship's nationality—for instance, either *G* or *M* for British, *K* or *W* for American—and the remaining letters complete the ship's name, which is also the radio call. United States naval vessels use *N* as the first letter of their calls. Originally the name signal and the radio call differed. In 1933 new radio call signals as listed in *MVUS* replaced the old name signals. Each issue of *MVUS* carries an appendix of United States call signs, consisting of four-letter *K* signals for large ships and two-letter-and-four-digit *W* signals for smaller craft, equipped only with radiotelephone. Since its edition of 1874 Lloyd's has shown, with the alphabetical entry for each ship, what it was beforehand in calling the "International Code of Signal Letters" now simply the call sign for all the world's shipping. The International Telecommunications Union issues an annual list of ship call signs.

One difficulty with all flag signals is that in darkness, in a calm, or with the relative wind direction unfavorable for the viewer, signals cannot be distinguished. Consequently ship name signals or any code signal may be transmitted visually in the international code by hoist combinations of lights for night-time use or of balls, cones, and cubes (which appear the same from any side view) for daytime use.

50. Name Badges

The name badge, or crest, is another type of surrogate naming. With the disappearance of figureheads, fancy scrollwork, gold leaf ,and other decorative features, the badge has become increasingly popular. Obviously, it satisfies the timeless desire of owners, captains, and companies to personalize their vessels. These badges are of two types according to location.

The first type appears high on the prow of merchant ships. The design may suggest the name or incorporate the printed name or initial. Often it is a sort of owner's trademark, appearing on all ships of his fleet and sometimes also used as a stack symbol and a flag design. Ordinarily the badge is painted directly on the prow, perhaps with features outlined by weld-beading, but it may be cut or cast in metal and attached. Typically, the badge is eighteen to thirty-six inches across and often is centered with several horizontal stripes or streamers extending back along each bow. Although the design of the badge may be free form, it is usually contained within a circle, a shield, or other regular shape.

Since about 1936 the Fred Olsen vessels of Norway have had attractive cast prow ornaments. These modern figureheads convey emblematically the ship names, all beginning with *B*, or have some association with those names. Thirty of these Olsen decorations are pictured in *The Decorative Arts of the Mariner*.[1]

The second type of decorative name badge appears elsewhere than on the prow. Its purpose is less for identification than to develop esprit de corps. Badges of this type are rare on merchant ships, although a few are said to exist. But vessels of various navies do have such badges, both official and unofficial, including many but not all ships of the Royal Navy, the British dominions, France, and the United States. The badge may be painted somewhere on the structure or on boards, carved from wood, cast in bronze, or emblazoned on flags.

On British ships the name badge often appears duplicated in various locations, such as in the vicinity of the quarterdeck, at the head of companionways, on battle-honor plaques, on gun tampions, and on ship's boats. *Heraldry in the Royal Navy* by Alfred E. Weightman illustrates over 300 of these official badges, all with the name as part of the design.[2] According to Weightman, use of the badges may have originated in the desire of officers ranking lower than admiral to identify their small boats. The badge gradually came into wider use aboard ship and eventually appeared on stationery and the like. An extension of the use is in the badges at the ends of pews and on the stained glass windows of the war memorial at Chatham.

Although used unofficially on various Royal Navy ships from about 1850, badges came into official use for qualifying vessels in 1918. By 1948 shapes became standardized as circular, pentagonal, shield, and diamond (all surmounted by a crown) for various types of warships. Sizes vary from $26\frac{1}{2}$ inches high for capital ships down to $15\frac{3}{8}$ inches high for destroyers, while the badges for ship's boats (though not limited to such use) range from 7 inches down to $5\frac{1}{2}$ inches. Responsibility for the designs now belongs to the College of Heralds. Previously, the commanding officer or ship's company determined the design. Accordingly it might change with command or for other reasons, as it did eight times in the case of the battleship *Africa* (1905).

Even though the ship name appears on the badge, the relationship of the name to the rest of the design is not always clear. An ark with a crown readily suggests *Ark Royal*, but a sprig of mustard for *Zest* is less obvious, and the cross flory from Nelson's arms for *Trafalgar* is even more obscure.

In the United States Navy the use of individual unit insignia, as for flotilla or squadron, dates at least from the 1930s, according to Captain J. H. B. Smith of the Naval History Division, who supplied most of the information on this subject. Badges apparently were first adopted by air squadrons and submarine units. During World War II widest use was by naval aircraft, submarine, Seabee, and motor torpedo boat units. Although the insignia were mostly group or command type, individual insignia also appeared on some large surface ships and probably on a few small ones. Until 1956, however, such devices had no official sanction and, in fact, were definitely discouraged for a time after the war, partly because they often incorporated unsuitable cartoon characters. When it was realized that badges had value in promoting ship and unit pride, their use gained approval. Eventually, most ships adopted individual name badges, which became official upon approval of the design, usually by the local fleet commander. These badges are used in addition to command type insignia. The latter are developed at command level and submitted to command members for comments and approval before being submitted via the administrative chain of command for official approval. The Naval History Division has a collection of over 1,000 ship and other unit insignia.

Badge content is only broadly guided by high authority. Designs must be in good taste and in keeping with naval tradition. Cartoon portrayals are to be avoided or limited. Heraldic designs are encouraged, as are designs symbolic of mission or history. The use of terse and appropriate mottoes is advised. Copyrighted designs may not be used. Finally, the designs should have good visibility. Shape of the badge is not specified for ships.

Currently, contrasting with British practice, a United States ship's badge may not be displayed on the ship's exterior except at the quarterdeck and on the gangway. Use of badges on unofficial stationery, plaques, jacket patches, decals, cigaret lighters, and the like is universal. The presentation of a ship or unit insignia on a plaque to domestic or foreign dignitaries or organizations is a common practice.

A typical United States Navy badge on the Polaris submarine *Daniel Boone* features a woodsman's long rifle and powderhorn on a red-white-and-blue shield, along with the motto "New Trails to Blaze." That for the destroyer *Frank E. Evans* is also essentially shield shaped and includes in the design a red fighting cock on a compass rose to match the motto "The Fighter." Since destroyer names honor naval heroes, elements of the family arms of the hero are sometimes incorporated in the design. Probably few badges would convey the names if they were not spelled out as part of the design; many badges also show the surrogate name, that is, the official letter-numeral combination. While the intent is for designs to continue meaningful over long periods, a design may be changed, as after modification of a ship.

Less widespread in the navy is the use of ship or other unit flags. Where these do exist, they may feature the name badge enlarged or merely the name. During World War II many submarines had battle flags showing the insignia and a miniature Japanese flag for each enemy ship sunk. As a sidelight on name flags, several flag histories affirm that the flag design adopted in 1917 by the State of Arizona had been that of the battleship *Arizona,* although naval files do not confirm this.[3] (For an early American use of individual warship flags for signal purposes, see the section on "Surrogate Names.)

51. Heraldic Names

Whereas the name badge was designed to suggest an existing ship name, the heraldic ship name was taken from existing armorial bearings. In the sixteenth and seventeenth centuries, especially, a number of heraldic names appeared on English ships. Once such names became traditional through use on successive vessels, the heraldic connotation probably in most cases disappeared.

The Anderson lists of men-of-war and hired merchantmen contained several names obviously, and numerous names probably, of heraldic origin. Three good examples were *Three Ostrich Feathers* (1546), twenty-ton vessel in the reign of Henry VIII; *Black Spread Eagle,* bought in 1642–43 under Cromwell; and *Falcon in the Fetterlock* (see section on "Unusual Names").[1]

If the truth were known, a considerable number of war and merchant vessels with simple names of mammals, birds, flowers, and miscellaneous symbols commonly used in heraldry doubtless had their origin in armorial insignia. Ships abounded named for the unicorn, dragon, griffin, leopard, fox, hart, swan, cock, crane, lily, rose, and so on. More explicit than the foregoing, to all appearance, were *Black Cock* and *Golden Dove,* both merchantmen hired for naval service between 1649 and 1667; *Palm Tree,* prize hoy of 1665; and *Arms of Rotterdam,* taken as *Wapen van Rotterdam* from the Dutch in 1674.[2] That, in some cases, a name may merely have matched decorations on a vessel and not have come from official armorial bearings is of course possible.

Heraldic names on ships were surrogate names of a ruler, place, family, or individual. Sir Walter Raleigh owned *Roebuck* with a name from his crest, a name carried on in the navy, and a similar source provided another often used name, *Squirrel,* for the pinnace of Raleigh's brother-in-law Sir Humphrey Gilbert.[3] The latter lost his life while returning from the founding at Newfoundland in 1583 of the first English colony in North America.

Heraldic nomenclature must often have been political in nature, as when Drake changed his ship's name to *Golden Hind* after the crest of a financial partner.

CHAPTER VIII

Miscellany

52. *Superstitions*

A NAME having seven letters is supposedly desirable for a ship, especially if it has three of the letter *a*, for example, *Arcadia* (1954), the P. and O. vessel. *Niagara*, carried by four *Lloyd's* ships, and *Tamaroa* (1943), a United States Coast Guard cutter, are other instances, though it is not implied that any of these names was chosen because of superstition. Through Biblical use the number *seven* is endowed with special significance, suggesting fullness or completeness. Probably by chance, there are seven letters in the name *Fortuna*, Roman goddess of good luck. The value of three *a* letters might derive from the practice of repeating blessings and magical incantations three times for greatest effectiveness.

Probably by coincidence, of the twenty-seven ships on the 1595 voyage of Drake and Hawkins, seven, or 25 percent, had seven-letter names (though none had the triplet *a*).[1] For ship lists in general, however, such a high percentage of seven-letter names is far from typical. In fact, a random examination of such lists in English suggests nothing whatever of statistical significance.

A Great Lakes freighter *Mataafa* (1899), although having seven letters in her name, apparently had one too many of the letter *a*, for she was wrecked near Duluth in 1905 with the loss of nine lives.[2]

Merchant Sail cited two other superstitions, quite probably limited as to time or place.[3] One held that ship names beginning with *A* were unlucky, perhaps an extension of the belief that women's names (but not men's) starting with *A* meant bad luck. This might have related to the scarlet letter *A* of Hawthorne's mid-nineteenth-century New England novel of adultery. The other superstition caused some sailors to shun vessels named after men, apparently because masculine names were considered unsuitable for ships deemed to be feminine. However, since the names of famous men were acceptable, it is quite possible other masculine full names suggested ownership by an individual likely to be stingy or a captain likely to be harsh with sailors.

In the British navy, according to Captain Manning, the best known ship superstition involves snake names, probably occasioned by the loss in modern times of *Cobra*, *Viper*, and *Serpent*. An outcry against naming a new submarine *Python* caused a change to *Pandora*, despite the fact

that over fifty Royal Navy ships with snake names suffered no disproportionate loss.[4]

During the wars with France, as Manning observed, the name of a ship
lost in action was assigned to a replacement. However, during World
War II the feeling developed that naming a ship after one sunk was unlucky, perhaps because replacements for both *Gurkha* and *Hardy* were
lost in turn. This naming practice was not eliminated, however, except in
the submarine service where the strong antipathy against it was re-
spected. As to the application of this superstition to merchant ships,
doubtless instances could be cited either way. At any rate, there is no
Titanic in *Lloyd's*.

Certain names are said to have been considered unlucky by Great
Lakes sailors, including *Oneida* (after an Indian tribe, a city, or a lake),
Racine (after a French poet or a city), and *Phoenix*. Around the turn of
the last century, twelve sail or steam ships—four with each of the aforementioned names—burned, foundered, struck reefs, or were lost in col-
lisions after unusually short lives on the Great Lakes. The vessels were of
varied types (a brig, schooners, paddlewheel and screw steamers, and
tugs) and all had different owners.[5]

Another name considered unlucky was *Melanope* (1876), a square-
rigger on which two captains committed suicide, one having first killed
his paramour who was sailing aboard and the other after his bride died
during their alcoholic honeymoon voyage. The ship was also involved in
mutiny, storm damage, and abandonment at sea before her final gasp as
a coal barge in the 1940s. When leaving Liverpool on her maiden voyage
she was cursed by a hag selling apples who had to be forced ashore.
Melanope is derived from the Greek *melanos*, meaning black or belonging to a dark class.[6]

On the other hand, some ships carried supposedly unlucky names
without apparent ill fortune. *Wandering Jew*, built in Camden, Maine,
was considered one of the smartest of ships in her day.[7] The name (also
that of a novel) recalls the legendary figure condemned to wander the
earth until Christ's Second Coming. Two American fishing boats, one
out of Seattle and the other out of Miami, were designated *Black Cat*.[8]

53. Name Changes

Another old superstition involves name changes. Although occasionally
mentioned in yachting circles, this appears to have little force today, especially if one judges by the section in *Lloyd's* listing the former names of

over 20,000 ships and the similar section in *MVUS68* showing the former names of over 36,000 ships. Moreover, many vessels have been renamed several times, some more than six times. Nevertheless, this superstition against renaming is not always ignored. In one view, name changing does not invite bad luck if ownership changes at the same time.

The Matson Line's *Malolo* (1927) had a series of minor mishaps while plying between San Francisco and Honolulu, which, according to waterfront gossip, occurred because the ship's name meant flying fish. Misusing the name of this fish, which had totemistic associations for native Hawaiians, was unlucky. The troubles ended once the name was changed to *Matsonia*.[1] However, there are those who say *Malolo*'s name was really changed because passengers nicknamed her "Maloler the Roller." When replaced by a new *Matsonia*, the old roller became the Greek *Queen Frederica*.

The belief that it is unlucky to change a ship's name has several possible origins. An ancient conception is that a name is an essential part of a thing, disclosing its place in the cosmos. Also, many ships are named for supernatural beings, whom it would be unwise to offend. Since name changing is often occasioned by smuggling or piracy or used to circumvent registry laws, authorities may have fostered the superstition.

On the other hand, there are always valid and sometimes pressing reasons for changing ship names. Personal names are often changed to conceal an unsavory past, to hide an ethnic origin, to carry on a family name, to mark a boy's puberty, to shed an embarrassing name or one difficult to spell or pronounce, or to adopt a name more suitable to a new station in life as in the case of a social climber, an actress, or a political leader. According to Noah J. Jacobs in *Naming Day in Eden*, to this day in Jewish tradition the name of a person critically ill is sometimes changed to confuse the Angel of Death.[2] In the case of first names, of course, the compelling reason for changing is simply that the individual dislikes the name given him.

With respect to the renaming of ships, a ship's past may be clouded by unfavorable publicity from mishap or litigation. Its name may be deemed unattractive to potential shippers or passengers, it may not fit a line's naming pattern, it may not suit some new use of the vessel, or it may be disliked by a new owner.

Basically, economics accounts for name changing of commercial ships. Ships go into new hands when shipowners die or retire, when recession eliminates marginal operators, when war or other events disrupt shipping routes and rates, when labor problems or political events or new taxes affect profits, and when newer type ships come into use. Some ships go to the scrapheap but most are acquired by other operators for use, perhaps in converted form, somewhere in the world.

Perhaps the earliest record of a name change involved the largest freighter known from antiquity, built by Hiero II (306–215 B.C.), who proudly named her after his city in Sicily, calling her *Syracusia*, translated *Lady of Syracuse* in the Loeb Classical Library version of *The Deipnosophists* by Athenaeus.[3] Upon learning that the draft of this great ship would exclude her from intended ports of call, Hiero renamed her *Lady of Alexandria* (*Alexandris*) and presented her to King Ptolemy of Egypt. This vessel, having a tonnage perhaps comparable to the United States frigate *Constitution*, was one of the earliest merchant ships of known name, a geographical name originally and a politicogeographical one after renaming.

An extreme, but not unique, instance of how often a ship's name and nationality may change involves the steamer originally called *Norseman*, built in Scotland in 1893 as a cableship for the Western and Brazilian Telegraph Company and after 1907 employed as a freighter until 1953. Dr. John Lyman, University of North Carolina, traced this ship through Lloyd's registers and elsewhere. The original name commemorated an earlier cableship sold after storm damage in 1892. How the second *Norseman* went through a gamut of thirteen typical ship names under ten different flags, over a sixty-year period, is summarized as follows:

1. *Norseman* (general proper noun) 1893, Great Britain
2. *Norse* (adjective) 1904, Great Britain
3. *Monte Blanco* (geographical) 1907, probably Callao, Peru
4. *Rimac* (Peruvian place name) perhaps 1909, Callao
5. *Monte Blanco* (geographical) perhaps 1913, Callao
6. *Inca* (general proper noun) date uncertain, probably Callao
7. *Tarapaca* (Chilean place name) perhaps 1916, Valparaiso, Chile
8. *Coronel* (Chilean place name) 1918, Valparaiso; 1918, Buenos Aires
9. *San Remo* (one of a French fleet of fifteen with Italian saints' names) 1921, Rouen, France; 1923, Genoa, Italy; 1925, owned by government of the Hedjaz; 1926, Beirut, Lebanon
10. *Riad* (*Riyadh*, Saudi Arabian place name) probably 1927, Alexandria, Egypt
11. *Adalet* (abstract name, "justice") probably 1932, Istanbul, Turkey
12. *Resit* (owner's first name) 1938, Istanbul
13. *Florya* (or *Flurya* for "chaffinch") 1940, Istanbul

While the vessel in the foregoing example had a new name, on the average, every 4½ years, more frequent changes are not unusual. Lloyd's registers showed that *Mission Santa Maria*, built in 1944 at Sausalito for the United States Maritime Commission), acquired nine names under seven flags in twenty-five years, which averages a change every 2¾ years.

Wholesale renaming sometimes occurs. In 1922 the United States Shipping Board renamed twenty-two ships for American presidents in one bureaucratic swoop.[4] (For the renaming by President Woodrow Wilson and his wife of former German merchant vessels seized when the United States entered World War I, see the section "Some Famous Namers.") In 1941 the United States took over about six dozen German and Italian vessels in American ports. Assigned to rename them, Lieutenant Commander W. C. Peet, Jr., chose names of past Kentucky Derby winners; *Man of War* went to a decrepit Italian tramp almost too tired to outsail a jellyfish.[5]

Two fine Hamburg-American passenger liners taken over as a consequence of World War I became famous under new names. *Vaterland* (1914), first interned and then seized at New York, transported troops as *Leviathan* and later became America's blue-ribbon liner. *Imperator* (1912), being larger and more luxurious than *Mauretania*, the old Atlantic queen, held the queen title briefly. Later as a war prize renamed *Berengaria* she carried British colors.[6]

The problem of naming a prize has often been resolved by modifying the old name of a captured vessel with the term *prize*. Not a modern practice, it certainly would not have been followed after World War II when the United States Coast Guard took over *Horst Wessel* (1933), having a name extolling a Nazi hero, as a training bark; the old name-board at the stern was simply turned over to expose a surface for the new name *Eagle*.[7] Another prize, *Atlantic*, a British letter-of-marque whaler taken in 1813 off the Galapagos Islands by the American *Essex*, was renamed *Essex Junior*.[8] This use of the *junior* suffix in a ship name may be unique.

Wartime prizes are not always renamed; some names are retained. Sometimes names are changed only in the sense of being translated: among illustrious English names, *Glory* had been *Gloire*, and *Renown* had been *Renommée*. Occasionally, some association with an old name is preserved, though obscurely: *Hébé* was renamed *Ganymede*, for the youth in mythology who succeeded Hébé as cupbearer to Zeus. The evolution of the puzzling name *Slothany* in English naval history becomes clear when it is realized this was originally *Slot van Honingen*, a Dutch prize taken in 1665.[9]

Not only conflict between nations but also upheaval within a nation leads to name changes. The Cromwellians dropped the *Saint* prefix wherever it existed in English ship names and altered all names suggesting royalty. *Prince Royal* became *Resolution*, until the return of Charles II restored the original name. Then, also, Cromwell's *Naseby* became *Royal Charles*, and *Winsby* became *Happy Return*.[10]

In a curious instance of renaming, the pirate Richard Worley in 1718 captured a Philadelphia sloop, which he renamed *New York Revenge*. Then, after taking *Eagle Galley* of London off the Virginia coast, Worley changed *Eagle's* name to *New York Revenge's Revenge*.[11]

Another piratical type, Count Felix von Luckner, sailed his *Sea Eagle* (*Seeadler*) under false Norwegian papers as *Irma*. *Sea Eagle*, originally the full-rigged British *Pass of Balmaha*, sank 100,000 tons of Allied shipping during World War I.[12]

Many famous ships originally carried different names. Captain James Cook's *Endeavour* had been the coastal collier *Earl of Pembroke* and eventually became the French whaler *Liberté*, while Cook's *Resolution* and *Adventure*, both also former colliers, had been respectively *Marquis of Granby* and *Marquis of Rockingham*.[13] Captain William Bligh's *Bounty* had been the merchant vessel *Bethina*.[14] Napoleon's flagship *Orient*, lost at the Battle of the Nile, had been laid down as *Le-Dauphin-Royal* and in 1795 had become *Sans-Culotte* (actually referring to men wearing long trousers instead of knee breeches).[15]

The tea clipper *Cutty Sark* (1869), as has frequently been related, had a figurehead of a bewitching female with a revealing garment, suggesting the fair young witch who danced in her outgrown chemise, or cutty sark, on Halloween in Burns's poem *Tam o'Shanter*. The ship also had scenes from the poem carved on bow and counter. In 1885, after having made the fastest wool passage from Australia, her owner gave her a cutty sark of gilded metal to go over the top of the maintruck. Later under Portuguese ownership *Cutty Sark*, although renamed *Ferreira*, usually was known as *Pequina Camisola*.[16] She is preserved in England under her original name. That her original owners, Willis and Son, also operated *Hallowe'en* (1870) is all but forgotten.[17] There was likewise a *Tam o'Shanter* (1866)[18] under different ownership (and, in fact, earlier and later ships with this same name); but John Willis, whose favorite poet was Burns, did install a figurehead of Tam o'Shanter on his favorite ship, *The Tweed*.

In at least two instances ships were renamed for reefs that brought them to grief. The sailing ship *Gainsborough* (1866), wrecked in 1898 on the reef at Diamond Head, received the name *Diamond Head* after being salvaged.[19] The four-masted bark *Pyrenees* (1891) from Glasgow, her grain cargo afire, purposely was run aground in 1900 on the lonely reef

Manga Reva several hundred miles from Pitcairn Island. Declared a complete loss, she nevertheless was later salvaged and renamed *Manga Reva* and had a useful life until lost at sea in 1917.[20]

Changing the name of a large modern ship, apart from altering all the legal and other records, involves considerable repainting. The name appears in three and sometimes four places on the hull. Usually the name also appears on a board at each side of the bridgehouse or directly on the superstructure, as well as on small boats and lifesaving gear, and perhaps on stationery, tableware, and other furnishings. What does not get changed, however, is the builder's plate, usually on the forward bulkhead of the bridgehouse. Frequently of bronze, this plate bears details of construction, tonnage, launch, and original name. Also remaining unchanged are the graffiti, consisting of the ship's name and usually a date and sometimes the home port, daubed in paint by crewmen on dock sides in various ports of the world. Occasionally, too, the ship's name is painted with care on some pier shed as a guide to where the ship's bridge should be positioned for best usage of bollards and cranes, though frequently a movable sign reading "bridge" serves that purpose.

54. Ship Surgery Names

Widespread use of welding on steel ships lends itself readily to ship surgery; that is, joining together sections from different ships or "jumboizing" to make ships longer.

King Saud I (*Al Malik Saud Al-Awal*, 1954), badly damaged in 1966 by fire and explosion, had her afterpart joined to the surviving forepart of *Anne Mildred Brovig* (1962), which had sunk off Heligoland. The resulting ore carrier bears the Norwegian name.[1]

In a different approach to naming a ship created in this manner, the British in 1941 assigned the name *Zubian* to the vessel produced by joining the bow portion of *Zulu* to the stern portion of *Nubian*.[2]

Nothing but confusion surrounds the name and legal status of *Observer*. The bow section of the Panama tanker *Wapello* (1953), built in the United States, was joined in Japan to the stern section of the Panama tanker *Esso Chittagong* (1943). The new tanker thus created was called *Santa Helena* and registered in Liberia. Then in 1966 *Santa Helena's* bow was fixed to the stern of *Trustco*, United States built and owned, to form *Observer*. The Supreme Court refused to decide whether *Observer* was a rebuilt *Trustco*, and thus qualified to engage in United States coastal trade, or a rebuilt *Santa Helena*, not qualified for such trade. The law requires that a vessel in coastal trade must have been built, registered, and owned in the United States. At last report the status of *Observer* was still undecided.[3]

55. Yachts

In general, the various name types already discussed for naval and merchant vessels will also be found on yachts. These include person names, place names, thing names, abstract names; simple and compound names; traditional and contemporary names; names from mythology and comic pages; foreign names and many more. Considered in their entirety, yacht names, as compared with those of merchant ships, differ mainly in tone or mood. Yachts being smaller and used for pleasure, this difference is to be expected.

Although the history of boats kept strictly for pleasure is comparatively short, if we except the watercraft of rulers and occasionally nobles, the diversity of yacht names is probably greater than that of naval or commercial vessels. Nobody knows how many yachts exist today in English-speaking countries, much less in the world. In the United States alone, the number of pleasure craft with inboard power is estimated to exceed 600,000, and that is also the approximate number for sailboats without power. What a lot of names!

Perhaps 95 percent of pleasure boats are owned by fairweather sailors, some of whom relax aboard but seldom leave the mooring or slip. Understandably, persons who have never experienced the real hostility of the sea and never learned to respect a boat often tend to select names quite different from those on commercial vessels.

Yacht names frequently have pleasant, carefree, romantic associations. *Windsong, Concerto, Coquette, Siren, Endless Summer*, and similar names are seen everywhere. Escape names include *Restless, Vagabond, Recluse, Therapy, Anodyne, Placebo, By Myself*, and *Serenity*. There are never-never-land names, bird names, fish names, cloud names, and many more. No possible play upon the words *lazy, sea, girl, Miss,* and *lady* has been overlooked.

Among clever names are puns (*SawSea*), words spelled backward (*Notsob*), words compounded from letters or syllables of family members (*Marjotom*), attempts at humor (*No More Golf*), alcoholic drinks (*Martini*), cartoon characters (*Snoopy*), and words like *Legacy* and *Windfall*. There are also slang terms (*Hang Up*), inside jokes such as that referring to bankruptcy (*Chapter Eleven*), occupational names

(*Law Office*), foreign words and phrases (including names too ribald to express in English), and even the name of the bull that killed Manolete (*Islero*).

A few racing sailboat skippers select names for the effect on competitors when seen from behind, such as *After Me* and *Adios*. I saw a large ocean catamaran with one hull labeled *Gary's Half* and the other hull *Bob's Half*. One trend is to use associated names, humorous if possible, for yacht and dinghy or tender, such as *Last Resort* and *Very Last Resort* or *Mistress* and *Love Child*.

Sailboat nomenclature tends to be less flip, more poetic, more traditional than powerboat nomenclature, although all kinds of names are found on both types of yachts, including names that were old long before the birth of Christ.

To determine how various name types range statistically, four volumes of *Lloyd's Register of American Yachts* (including Canadian) for the years 1939, 1950, 1960, and 1970 were examined.[1] The first entry was noted from each page having a number ending in *0* or *5*. The sample was 464 names, or roughly 1.3 percent of total entries. It must be realized, of course, that each yacht register included little more than 1 percent of American yachts, although it listed a higher percentage of large ones. Nonetheless, the names in the register and the sampling may be taken as fairly representative, as confirmed by observation of names on actual transoms.

One usage disclosed in the register, however, probably was not typical: eighty-eight names of the sample, or 19 percent, were followed by a roman numeral (II, III) to indicate successive use of the same name, almost always by the same owner or family. Some yachtsmen avoid such usage as seeming boastful, but obviously this sentiment is not widespread. In place of the roman numeral some yachts use the word *Two* or *Too* or even a foreign *Dos* or *Deux*. The roman numeral is seldom used on merchant vessels; occasionally, the word *New* will precede the original name, but this too is infrequent.

Names of yachts also differ noticeably from those of merchant ships in the frequency of person-name acronyms. Such acronyms apparently compounded of two names totaled forty and of three names fifteen in the sample, or fifty-five in all for about 12 percent. These acronyms apparently reached a peak of popularity in 1950 when the total was three times greater than in 1970. Many of these names are hard, if not impossible, to analyze.

Apart from the probable decline in the use of acronyms, significant percentage shifts over the years were not apparent in the other categories tabulated. Predictably, the largest category was for feminine names, mostly specific ones but also including *Ballerina, Huntress, Our Lady,* and *Texas Queen.* These totaled eighty-five, or about 19 percent. The next largest category comprised forty-five names suggesting romance and escape—*Daydream, Escapade, Fun, Sinbad,* and *Water Gypsy.* Foreign language words totaled about twenty, perhaps more if some seemingly made-up words were included. Bird names numbered seventeen, not all of them bird-book species. Fourteen names were borrowed from ships of the past, fifteen if one includes *L'Ark.* Geographical words constituted only eleven in the sample, not quite 2.5 percent, an insignificant number when compared with the many geographical names on large merchant vessels. Musical terms tallied five. Only three names were of specific men.

The rest of the names in the sample, 174 in all, were difficult to categorize. Some appeared to be made-up names, but what they were was uncertain—foreign words, fictional names, unusual person names, acronyms, lispings, or flights of fancy? Most of the 174 names, however, consisted of a variety of terms best indicated by the following examples: *Black Watch, Bittersweet, Buccaneer, Dauntless, Foxfire, Kelpie, Meerschaum, Moby Dick, Privateer, Saunterer, Show Boat, The Most, Twang, Welcome, Whistlepitcher,* and *Yawl Kitten.*

Name changes for yachts are probably more frequent than for merchant ships. The 1939 yacht register contained about 6,860 entries and an appendix of about 4,600 former names; the same figures for the 1970 edition are about 11,500 and 9,500. There is no accounting for taste when one sees *Shearwater* changed to *Black Crow, Thistle* to *Shank's Mare,* and *Float* to *Nux Vomica.*

For some persons the selection of a name must be difficult. Otherwise there would be no profit from a yachting magazine advertisement offering a list of 5,000 names for one dollar, names said to be suitable for anything afloat from a dinghy to a battleship.

56. *"Maru"*

While the origins of *maru* are lost in antiquity, the use of this word by the Japanese has broadened through the centuries.[1] Today it has well over a dozen meanings, several of them slang. That is why one gets different and usually wrong answers from Japanese mariners as to the meaning of the term in the names of their vessels.

Most of the meanings of *maru* seem to derive from the circle: from the circle as such, from drawing a circle, or from circumscribing something. Since the circle in the Orient symbolizes perfection, completeness, or entirety, *maru* also carries that connotation.

Adding it as a suffix to a child's name made the name an affectionate diminutive and expressed the pride, the hope, and the expectation that the samurai felt for the heir. As a suffix in an adult name *maru* implied a compliment. With time *maru* was sometimes added to the name given worthy inanimate objects, perhaps to a trusty sword or to a castle circumscribed by a wall (as by a circle). Such usages connoted not only value and completeness but also strength and protection. So understandably the term seemed appropriate for a warship, which was a sort of floating castle. As used in ship names, it might be said that *maru* adds a meaning rather like the English expression "the good ship So-and-So."

The first ship on which the term was used is believed to have been the warship *Nippon Maru* (1591), and from then on it appeared on all warships until the practice was discontinued about 1869. Meanwhile, *maru* was adopted for commercial vessels and continues in use today. However, some Japanese shipping lines use Westernized names, such as those of the container ships *Golden Gate Bridge* (1968) and *Japan Ace* (1969). The Westernization of Japan and the increasing use of foreign registry for Japanese ships is hastening the abandonment of *maru*.

Japan Line, the first to eliminate the use of *maru* entirely, may also be the first shipping company with stock not closely held to permit its stockholders to share in ship naming. When Japan Line adopted the policy of using flower names for tankers and tree names for dry cargo ships, its stockholders by vote chose as the first such names *Japan Lily* (1965), *Japan Rose* (1965), *Japan Pine* (1965), and *Japan Elm* (1965).[2]

CHAPTER IX

Namers

57. Ships That Gave Their Names

WHILE ships without number have taken geographical names, relatively few have given their names to features on charts today. Explorers tend to name features after persons (sovereigns, friends, financial backers, fellow officers, themselves), after places in their homelands, or after some incident or observation at the name location. Nevertheless, all round the world, ship names are to be found as place names.

The Columbia River recalls *Columbia* (1787), the vessel that discovered its mouth and was also the first American ship to circle the globe (1788–90).[1] Just 200 years earlier an English ship gave her name to Port Desire; Thomas Cavendish in 1588 with *Desire* and another vessel lost half his men in traversing the Strait of Magellan. And about ten years earlier than *Desire's* ordeal, the name of one of Frobisher's vessels was given to Gabriel Island in Frobisher Bay and to Gabriel Strait not far away. Gabriel Strait lies between Baffin Island and Resolution Island in northeastern Canada, the latter being named for one of the ships in which Thomas Button explored Hudson Bay. Off the southwest coast of New Zealand lies another Resolution Island, named for Cook's ship of that name. That great navigator also gave ship names to Endeavour River in northeast Australia, to Endeavour Strait between New Guinea and Australia, and to Adventure Bay at the southeast tip of Australia.

The Russian navigator Otto Kotzebue made the Marshall Islands known to the world, and Rurik Passage marks the course his ship *Rurik* took in entering Christmas Harbor at the Wotje atoll.[2] About sixty years later a Russian corvette sailed between New Guinea and New Britain, and this ship is remembered by Vitiaz Passage.[3] Captain Mertho, the Englishman who discovered Kwajalein in the Marshalls, sailed in *Ocean* and probably also found and named Ocean Island.[4] Pitt Strait off New Guinea bears the name of the East Indiaman under Captain Wilson which challenged Dutch supremacy by sailing from India to China.

On the western shores of North America the name of George Vancouver's sloop was assigned to Discovery Island at the Strait of Juan de Fuca, to Discovery Passage off Vancouver Island, and to nearby Mount Discovery. Vancouver's lieutenant on the accompanying armed tender

Chatham named Chatham Island off New Zealand after his vessel. There is also Chatham Strait near Prince Rupert, British Columbia.

About 500 miles southeast of New Zealand lie the Bounty Islands. Captain Bligh's ship, taken by the mutineers, also is remembered by Bounty Trough.

Lying between Baffin Island and mainland Canada, Cape Fury and Hecla Strait recall the two vessels *Fury* and *Hecla* on which William Parry's party spent two winters in Foxe Basin.[5] Beagle Channel in the Strait of Magellan about eighty miles north of Cape Horn was discovered by Captain Robert Fitzroy on the *Beagle* expedition just prior to that on which Darwin made observations leading to his famous theory.[6]

A study of charts and records discloses many shoals, banks, points, mountains, and other geographical features bearing ship names. Ships wrecked on reefs and rocks have, understandably, through popular usage bequeathed their names to the hazards that often sealed their fate. For example, Sacramento Reef off Baja California caused the loss in 1872 of the Pacific Mail steamer *Sacramento* (1864) and marooned 145 passengers on waterless Geronimo Island for about a week. At Bishop Rock, a submerged peak in Cortez Bank about 100 miles west of San Diego, the Philadelphia-built clipper *Stillwell S. Bishop* (1851) scraped disaster but did make it safely to San Francisco after putting in at San Diego.[7] Queen's Gate marks the entrance to a safe haven, Long Beach harbor, and was so named when that California city acquired the venerable *Queen Mary*. Discovery Deep, the Atlantis II Deep, and the Chain Deep are deep pools of hot brine in the Red Sea named for the oceanographic ships that located the pools between 1957 and 1966.[8]

Apart from the enduring geographical names that preserve certain ship names for posterity, other ships, especially the famous clippers, have loaned names to pubs, bottled goods, a hair style, and even a baby. Doubtless *Cutty Sark* is better known as a whiskey than as a ship. Both a San Diego saloon and a nearby gold mine were named for *Oriflamme*, a wooden sidewheeler that once plied California coastal waters.[9] *Belle Poule*, French victor in a 1778 engagement with the British, gave her name soon thereafter to a high hairdress topped with a small model of a full-rigged ship, *a la Belle Poule*.[10] Few persons realize that the name *Cleopatra's Needle* for the obelisk of Thutmose III in London does not refer directly to the Egyptian queen but rather to the curiously shaped vessel *Cleopatra* that was built around the obelisk at Alexandria in order to transport it to London on a voyage requiring four months.[11] A baby was named for a ship that had been named for a war hero. In 1942, during World War II, *City of New York* (1930) became a U-boat victim off

North Carolina. Among the passengers was the pregnant wife of the Yugoslav consul at New York, a Mrs. Mohorovicic, who gave birth in a crowded lifeboat. Later, when introduced to the captain of a rescuing American destroyer, she announced she would give the destroyer's name to her son, who thus became Jesse Roper Mohorovicic.[12]

While a ship name may be borrowed by a pub, the reverse may also be true. Captain Charles Allers commanded a nameless trading schooner on the Great Lakes about 1880. The story goes that one day upon entering a Chicago waterfront saloon he saw one name on the window, but when he departed he saw two. So he took one name for his schooner, which thereafter was *X-10-U-8*, pronounced "Extenuate."[13]

Throughout naval history there has been a tendency to identify a naval ship's company by the name of the ship. As previously mentioned, Imperial Rome assigned the ship's name to the ship's company, and this may sometimes have been the practice in ancient Egypt. In the British and American navies of the late eighteenth and well into the nineteenth century, a ship's company was often informally known by the plural form (or sometimes in the case of a compound name by the plural form of the key word) of the warship's name. For instance, in an exhortation delivered to the crew of the British vessel *Shannon* (1806), while clearing for action against the United States frigate *Chesapeake* (1799) in June of 1813, the captain addressed his men familiarly as "Shannons."[14] Not only naval officers, of course, but naval seamen as well sometimes used this nomenclature in referring to themselves or men from other ships.

58. Some Famous Namers

Who selects a ship's name seldom gets recorded. Ordinarily, for commercial ships the namer is the owner. For state-owned vessels name selection is usually a bureaucratic process, beginning with some obscure underling whose proposals go up the line for consideration, perhaps even as high as the nation's ruler. Sometimes a favored captain is permitted the choice. Again, the namer may be the shipbuilder, the banker, the owner's wife or relatives or employes, or even as in the case of Japan Line the public stockholders. The ship is fortunate when the responsible party is sensitive to the psychological importance of a good name.

Sir Francis Drake, while at Port Saint Julian in South America, decided to change *Pelican* to *Golden Hind*. This was a compliment to Sir Christopher Hatton, a partner in Drake's venture, whose arms included a heraldic hind.[1]

Drake's queen assigned *Elizabeth Jonas* (1559) to her new sixty-four gun warship, for the reason, as explained in Holinshed's *Chronicles*, that she was delivered like Jonas from the belly of the whale to confound her enemies. Before the actual christening, the ship was tentatively called *Peter* and then *Edward*.[2] Gustavus Adolphus of Sweden, another royal namer, gave his dynasty name to *Vasa*, the highly decorated warship recently salvaged from Stockholm harbor where she capsized on her maiden voyage in 1628.[3] With *Loyal London*, named by the king in appreciation of the construction funds supplied by citizens of that city, Charles II was not more fortunate than the Swedish king, for the vessel was soon lost, and the Londoners were not minded to repeat their generosity.[4]

Charles II and his brother James II, both greatly interested in naval affairs, named or renamed many English ships. As pointed out in *BWN*, the hand of the king may be assumed in numerous instances, including *Royal Oak* (1664), for the hollow tree that sheltered him during his flight from the field in 1651, and *Royal Escape*, acquired in 1660 as a royal yacht, which as the brig *Surprise* had carried him into exile nine years earlier. Ships named for Charles's mistresses and illegitimate sons included, in the first category, *Cleveland, Portsmouth,* and *Fubbs*; and in the second, *Grafton, Lennox, St. Albans,* and *Monmouth. Fubbs* was the king's pet name for the Duchess of Portsmouth and came from the English word *fubby* meaning plump, fair.

John Paul Jones chose the name *Bon Homme Richard*—in tribute to Benjamin Franklin ("Poor Richard")—for the former French East Indiaman *Duc de Duras*.[5]

George Washington named a number of United States ships, including what many consider to have been the nation's first warship, the frigate called *Constellation* (1797) after the blue field with stars of the national flag. Actually the name was one of ten names proposed by Secretary of War Timothy Pickering for the fleet of five frigates then under construction and temporarily designated *A* through *E*. The proposals were *United States, Constitution, President, Congress, Constellation, Defender, Fortitude, Perseverance, Protector,* and *Liberty*. Washington chose the first five.[6]

Napoleon renamed the prize brig *Speedy* and presented her as *San Pietro* to Saint Peter's successor, Pius VII.[7]

Donald McKay knew that a good ship deserves a good name and was permitted to name as he pleased certain clippers from his yard, including *Flying Fish* (1852), a name that recalls the story of a New Bedford ship captain, who later was harbormaster for the port of New York.[8] This captain was hailed by a revenue cutter while on a trading voyage to the West Indies during the 1830s.

"What's the name of that brig?"

"*Flying Fish.*"

"What cargo?"

"Pickled fish."

"Captain's name?"

"Preserved Fish."

Flushed and angry, the revenue cutter captain boarded the brig to deal with the joker, only to find proof that every word was true. Preserved Fish, furthermore, claimed an ancestor of the same name who was a Revolutionary War general.

Among other ships believed to have been named by McKay were *Flying Cloud* (1851), *Sovereign of the Seas* (1852), *Lightning* (1854), *Stag Hound* (1850), *Westward Ho* (1852), *Romance of the Seas* (1853), and *Glory of the Seas* (1869), all memorable choices. McKay's own name was chosen by James Baines for one of the four McKay clippers launched for the English company, 1854–55. Baines assigned his own name to one clipper that had his likeness as a figurehead. He wanted a figurehead of McKay on *Donald McKay* (1855), but the shipbuilder refused, ordering instead a figurehead of a Scot wearing the McKay tartan.[9] McKay could not have been pleased by names given to two ships he built for Zerega and Company, New York. One was *A.Z.* (1847), 675 tons; the other, *L.Z.* (1848), 897 tons. The merchant heading the Zerega firm kept no books, put nothing in writing, and obviously believed in brevity.[10]

Winston Churchill was among the most illustrious ship namers of this century. During World War I as first lord of the Admiralty he found himself in conflict with George V over ship names, as related by Vice Admiral Gretton in *Former Naval Person*.[11] Among the names Churchill proposed were *Assiduous, Liberty*, and *Oliver Cromwell*. The first name obviously invited ribald nicknames and the second vulgarization as "Libertine"; the third was the name of a regicide. The King, who had a sense of fitness from his naval background, rejected all three names but softened his rejection by including the name of the first Churchill among his alternate suggestions, which were *Marlborough, Delhi,* and *Wellington*. The ships finally became *Marlborough* (1912), *Emperor of India* (1913), and *Iron Duke* (1912); presumably Churchill suggested the substitutions for two of the royal proposals.

On *Oliver Cromwell*, however, Churchill would not give up. He proposed it again the following year. Having no intention of naming a ship after a regicide, the king again rejected the name in a pointed note alluding to his previous rejection. Nothing daunted, Churchill twice more urged the name, the last time submitting quotations from historians extolling Cromwell's contribution to the navy and concluding with the tactless statement: "It certainly seems right that we should give to a battleship a name that never failed to make the enemies of England tremble." The King stood grimly firm, however. The name *Valiant* (1914) was then submitted and accepted as a substitute. The King also rejected the proposed *Pitt,* for the very good reason that the name invited a vulgar rhyming nickname.

During World War II, in order to deny enemy intelligence information on numbers and types, British submarines were identified only by code letters and numbers, but those in the submarine service began to use unofficial names regardless. When this situation came to the attention of Churchill as prime minster, he ordered that all submarines were to be officially named immediately, and he himself supplied two names, *Tiptoe* (1944) and *Varangian* (1943).[12] *Tiptoe* probably carried the figurative meaning of eagerly expectant as applied to those aboard or of stealthy or silent approach, characteristic of a submarine. *Varangian,* referring to the Norse bodyguards in the service of the Byzantine emperor, suggests that she may have been manned by non-British volunteers.

Churchill was not the only naval person whose suggestions were sometimes rejected. At the time of the Spanish-American War, some ranking individual in the United States Navy, having decided that American colleges should be honored afloat, rechristened two British-built armed auxiliaries *Yale* and *Harvard.* When Admiral George Dewey took several Spanish warships in the Battle of Manila Bay, he was directed from Washington to give them college names. The admiral wryly proposed *Massachusets Institute of Technology* and *Vermont Normal College for Women.*[13]

The selection of a suitable name may require much thought or may come in a flash. Mrs. Woodrow Wilson studied mythology and dictionaries for several weeks after being asked by the United States Shipping Board to rename *Vaterland* (1914), Germany's pride taken over in World War I. Still the president's wife could not decide upon a name for what was then the world's largest ship. When she approached her husband, he had no such trouble but responded at once: "*Leviathan,* the monster of the deep; it's in the Bible."[14]

In her autobiography Mrs. Wilson tells the story somewhat differently. When the chairman of the Shipping Board, Edward N. Hurley, asked her to rename eighty-eight German vessels taken over in United States ports, she went over the list with the president and exclaimed over the tonnage of *Vaterland*. He promptly said, "Well, that one is easy, for it would have to be the *Leviathan*." He also named the smallest *Minnow*. Mrs. Wilson retained the original German names of *President Lincoln, President Grant*, and *George Washington* and anglicized the spelling of *America*. That left eighty-two ships to be given names. "I started to use the names of American cities, rivers, lakes, mountains and so on," Mrs. Wilson wrote, "and was surprised to find that most of them had been previously used. So I returned to Indian names, which had really been my first idea, but discarded because most of them were long and hard to spell. There seemed, however, no recourse. This rather than the fact that I myself am of Indian descent, explains the use of Indian names."[15] Mrs. Wilson was next asked by Hurley to name hundreds of new merchant ships. She obtained Indian dictionaries from the Library of Congress and pressed her brother into service. "Trivial as it may seem," she wrote, "as the War went on, and other duties increased, this work of naming ships became a genuine burden." She both named and christened the first ship to leave the ways at Hog Island, calling it *Quistconck* (1918), which meant Hog Island in one of the Indian tongues.[16]

The American president, Richard M. Nixon, personally named the nuclear aircraft carrier *Dwight D. Eisenhower* after the man he served under as vice-president; and he assigned his son-in-law, David Eisenhower, the former president's grandson, to officiate at the keel-laying of the 500-million-dollar behemoth.

59. Fictional Ships, Mostly Real Names

Some imaginary ships of literature seem more real than actual ships of history. An author's imagination may act upon his knowledge of real ships to produce a work of art convincing to the reader, who vicariously grips a shroud during a bitter gale, participates in a stirring sea fight, or hearkens to the creak of tackle and the swish of the sea. The most convincingly real of these imaginary vessels always have names, mostly real names, that contribute to the impression of realism. Sometimes the name is imaginary, too, but more often the author, consciously or otherwise, uses the name of an actual ship.

Hispaniola was apparently a fictional name; at least it was not found in Lloyd's registers published around 1881 when Stevenson was writing *Treasure Island*. As the anglicized version of the name given by Columbus to the island later called Santo Domingo and now again Hispaniola, it was an apt name suggesting pirates roving the Spanish main.

Less imaginary was the name of Captain Ahab's *Pequod* out of Nantucket, her tiller made from the jawbone of a whale. *Pequod* was Melville's variant of an actual ship name, *Pequot,* designating an extinct tribe of New England Indians. *Moby Dick* appeared in 1851; Lloyd's registers listed a Maine *Pequot* of 1846 and another of 1852.

While a resident of Vermont, Kipling wrote *Captains Courageous* and not improbably knew of the fifty-six-ton *We're Here* that sailed out of Beverly, Massachusetts, because he assigned this name to the fishing schooner in the story.[1] Kipling also wove ship names into the meter of his verses titled *Minesweepers, 1914,* in which he extolled the British fishermen whose trawlers swept the fairways for the safety of merchant ships during World War I. Each stanza ends with a line listing the trawlers: *Unity, Claribel, Assyrian, Stormcock,* and *Golden Gain. Unity II* (1904) and *Golden Gain* (1913) were actual drifters and *Stormcock* (1892) a trawler.[2] Probably the others existed, too.

Jules Verne must have had Robert Fulton's three-man submarine in mind when he chose *Nautilus* for his wonderful undersea craft.

John Masefield's *Wanderer*, "the loveliest ship my eyes have ever seen," had her namesake in the four-masted British bark built in 1891, which made a fast run from the Golden Gate to Queenstown harbor in 107 days.[3] In *Ships,* another poem, Masefield threaded through his couplets the names of thirty-seven ships, all of which, from *Argus* (probably the ship of 1879, Glasgow) to *Yola* (probably the iron schooner of 1879, London), were very likely the names of actual vessels.

Like many another boy, young Joseph Conrad apparently was inspired to go to sea by reading Frederick Marryat's *Peter Simple,* a novelized tribute to Lord Cochrane and his *Impérieuse* on which Marryat once served. *Diomede,* the name used in the novel, was a geographical name seemingly chosen because of its near identity to the mythological name *Diomedes* carried by several Royal Navy warships from 1781 onward.

Devotees of Conrad will recall the rusty old steamer *Patna,* carrying Arab pilgrims in *Lord Jim*; the steamer *Nan-Shan,* which barely survived in *Typhoon* with a cargo of coolies tumbling in the hold; and, of course, *Narcissus* (1876), the ship on which Conrad once served and from which he borrowed the name for use in *The Nigger of the "Narcissus,"* his elaboration of an incident supposed to have occurred on one of the several actual vessels called *Duke of Sutherland.* Another Conrad ship was *Sofala* in *End of the Tether,* a story deriving from a voyage he made as first mate of *Vidar.* Conrad usually identified his fictional ships in the very first sentence or at least in the first paragraph, for his ships were major characters.

By contrast, writers with little or no knowledge of the sea and with no awareness of the importance to the seafarer of a name, often immortalize anonymous vessels. Thus the Ancient Mariner who shot the albatross never named the ship on which all but him had perished. Nor did Robinson Crusoe name the 120-ton vessel that left him a castaway for so many years. (*Cinque Ports* was the real vessel that left Crusoe's prototype, Alexander Selkirk, on a lonely Juan Fernández island.) And the wrecked hulk that supplied the Swiss Family Robinson with so much to comfort them on their island was also nameless.

The sea is the principal villian and the flower-class corvette *Compass Rose* the principal heroine in *The Cruel Sea*, Nicholas Monsarrat's novel about Atlantic convoy duty during World War II. The writer selected corvette names so typical that one is surprised not to find them in the British section of *Jane's* wartime editions, names such as *Petal, Pergola*, and *Rose Arbour*. The frigate *Saltash*, the center of interest after the loss of *Compass Rose*, carried an old Royal Navy name, a geographical one, which in World War II was actually borne by a minesweeper.

Other ship names, a few among many, that either before or after their fictional use appeared on actual transoms, included the ill-starred *Good Fortune*, which stranded Enoch Arden on an uninhabited isle and confounded his marriage; *Ariel* of James Fenimore Cooper's tale *The Pilot*; *Antelope*, which carried Gulliver to his East Indian encounter with the Lilliputians; the cat-rigged *Marsh Duck*, on which the hero of *Islandia* sailed with the beauteous Dorna through the marshes of a Utopian land; and *African Queen*, the launch on which another couple, a roughneck mismatched with an old maid missionary, escaped down an African river in one of C. S. Forester's non-Hornblower novels.

CHAPTER X

Summing Up

60. Briefly Stated

CERTAIN aspects of ship naming can now be summarized. First of all, the practice of naming ships has a long history, certainly from about 2615 B.C. in Egypt and without doubt considerably earlier.

The oldest ship names probably were owner names in the wide sense of being owned by, and named for, a god, a community, a ruler, or a private individual. Quite possibly the first names developed from clan or god symbols of primitive communities.

Ships acquire names for several distinct reasons, usually mixed in practice: religious, to invoke the protection of supernatural beings; sentimental, involving emotion, fancy, pride of ownership; politicoeconomic, to help foster unity, pride, or prosperity and perhaps to impress potential enemies; and identification, to establish ownership and legal responsibility, assist in record keeping and the collection of taxes, and generally to further trade.

When the written name first came to be applied somewhere upon the ship remains unknown. There is a suggestion that some Egyptian stone-carrying craft of around 1500 B.C. had hieroglyphs to identify them, but the impression most widely held is that symbols were used to suggest ship names almost into modern times. To me it appears probable that for thousands of years written names have appeared on many large ships, often with name symbols for the unlettered, among all maritime peoples having a written language.

Name magic has been involved at times in the naming process because of the belief that power exists in a name. Knowing the true name of a god or creature was supposed to give power to the possessor of that secret.

Ship naming usually has been marked by religious ceremonies involving the sacrifice of persons, animals, or agricultural products; the libation of wine; or a solemn blessing similar to baptism.

Good names for ships should be easy to remember, easy to spell, easy to pronounce, harmonious in sound, agreeable in meaning. But many names not meeting these standards may nevertheless be good if they show respect for the vessel, a sense of fitness, perhaps a feeling for tradition. For those aboard a ship a good name is psychologically important, especially in wartime when a proud name may be the difference between victory and defeat.

A strong tradition is involved in ship nomenclature, one that carries along many very old names. In any given period new names having contemporary significance are infused. Some of these new names take their place in the long tradition, while others are soon forgotten.

Names preserved from ancient times were those of war craft or other vessels of state. Probably merchant vessels had names similar but less aggressive or grandiose. In certain periods, to be sure, the distinction between warships and merchantmen hardly existed.

Many old ship names from Egypt obviously reflected a certain political insecurity, a tendency for the Two Lands to snap apart. Hence names stressed unity, exalted pharaoh as a god-ruler, and upheld Amon as the national god.

Surviving Babylonian names, on the other hand, reflected no such political tensions. All were metaphorical names, applied to a number of gods.

Greek names from the third century B.C. showed the Greeks had salt-water in their blood; the names are indistinguishable from many names in modern registers.

Many of the old Roman names are likewise to be found on transoms today. These names were sober, including those of gods or personifications or places, and in general disclosed that Rome was primarily a land power concerned with maintaining stability in her world.

As names for their ships the Vikings favored compounds, as did the Egyptians and Babylonians. In the late pagan period the Vikings were fascinated by *orms*, formidable sea serpents or dragons. They gave *orm* names to ships, swords, spears, and strong men.

Early English names probably differed little in type from those of mainland Europe. Among the oldest on record were *Queen* and *Countess*, generic titles; and there were many owner names and religious names.

Certain god names have continued in use from earliest times. Fifty such names constituted about 0.66 percent of *Lloyd's* entries. Christianity introduced God, the Virgin, angels, and saints into ship nomenclature. Although names reflecting Christianity are far less numerous now than in earlier times, such entries in *Lloyd's* tallied not less than $1\frac{1}{2}$ percent of total entries.

The all-time favorite feminine name for ships in English, and probably throughout the Christian world in one or another of its variations, is *Mary*. Samplings of *MVUS68* showed that *Mary*, alone or in combination with a surname, comprised nearly 1 percent of total entries. *Elizabeth* or one of its diminutives was next with nearly 0.66 percent of entries. Feminine names as a whole constituted about 20 percent of *MVUS68* entries, but in George Washington's day feminine names totaled much higher.

Men's names have never been so popular as women's for ships, although they constituted roughly 10 percent of *MVUS68* entries. However, about a century ago in America, men's names appeared more frequently on sailing vessels; of 242 Down Easters, nearly 40 percent had men's names.

Geographical names form another large category. For Roman warships the place name was exceeded in popularity only by the god name. Of 196 square-rigged packets on transatlantic routes in the nineteenth century, about 38 percent had geographical names. A sampling of *MVUS68* suggested that place names now appear on about 12 percent of all registered American vessels, but the percentage may be twice that for large American and foreign ships calling at United States ports. The place name need not be a simple name, such as that of a city, but may be a compound in which the place appears in adjectival form. Also it may be a general term, such as *Arctic*, may refer to some ancient or imaginary place, or may suggest the whole by naming a part (*Acropolis*).

War and dissention have produced ships named for battles, for heroes, for such abstractions as liberty and freedom, or perhaps for some significant date. Names may also suggest revolt, revenge, defense, offense, and victory.

War names are political names of an extreme type, but sometimes the political name has been assigned in peacetime to further some goal—such as party power or national unity—or to compliment some person, minority group, city, or larger area. Likewise individual shipowners have selected names to flatter shippers, rulers, or trading country nationals.

Names stressing peace and friendship never go entirely out of style but proliferate most following periods of conflict, when traders want to soothe recent animosities and get back to the business of profits. Names suggesting safety, diligence, and profit appear to be chosen not only to invite custom but also perhaps in the hope of wish fulfillment.

Ship names may be classed as person names, place names, thing names, and abstract names. Person names include those of divinities, saints, rulers, heroes, folk characters, and persons connected in some way with ships. Place names are from the real or imaginary worlds. Thing names are most numerous of all, including those of animate and inanimate objects, real or imaginary, in bewildering variety. Abstract names express emotions, qualities, characteristics, and ideas.

Names are nouns, adjectives, verbs, or combinations of these, the noun being by far the most common. Use of the verb is infrequent. The adjective ship name, although used by the Greeks and having a long history in English, yet has a certain strangeness in English except when modifying a noun in a compound name. The adjective name probably was introduced into English about 1700 by the capture of French prizes.

The definite article *The*, while infrequently part of a ship name in English, has been an integral part of names in some countries.

Rather rare in English, except on tugs and barges, the numerical name has appeared occasionally on large ships. On small vessels it has had limited use in England and the United States, usually on naval craft. In Japan a line may use the same name for many ships, suffixing a differentiating numeral. Sailors have disliked the strictly numerical name.

Double names, such as *Philip and Mary*, have often been used and on American schooners were quite popular.

Paired names, such as *Saint Peter* and *Saint Paul*, associate two persons, places, things, or ideas for ships that voyage together or are under common ownership.

The series name now so widely used developed from paired names. Lines have used series names of gems, cities, castles, and so on; names beginning with the same letter or including a common word or ending in a common syllable. Apart from satisfying a sense of order or carrying out some owner's whim, series naming identifies ships of a particular line and perhaps attracts business.

Even if care is taken to give a ship a good name, which neither lends itself to punning nor suggests anything humorous or ribald, she may still acquire a nickname based on appearance or performance. The nickname need not be unsuitable, for example, *Old Ironsides*. Often a nickname is a feminized form of the owner's name, as was the case with *Niña* and *Pinta*, now only known by nicknames.

Despite the superstition against name changing, a great many ships have their names changed. This is done to conceal an unfavorable past, to fit a new naming pattern, to suit some new use of the vessel, or merely to satisfy an owner's preference. Seizure of ships in wartime has occasioned wholesale renaming. *Lloyd's* listed the former names of over 20,000 merchant and passenger ships.

While some yacht names are indistinguishable from those of naval or merchant vessels, other names suggest the carefree, the romantic, or the wanderer or are pun names or names composed of syllables from the names of family members. Other names may disclose the profession or interest of the yachtsman. Sailboats, which usually have traditional or poetic names, are less likely than small powerboats to display names that are flip or unusual.

Ships throughout history have had some very unusual names, indeed. However, unusual names may not be inappropriate unless they show complete disrespect, as in naming a ship for a soup pot or a rotten apple.

The same name often is carried by successive ships devoted to a specific purpose. For over 500 years the Egyptians had ships called *Amon Re in the Sacred Barge*. No name has been more favored by explorers than *Discovery*. Navies perpetuate illustrious names. Sometimes the cargo a ship carries is indicated by its name. Ships having a specific function, whether fighting fires or laying cables, often have been named to suit the function.

Many ships have given their names to rivers, islands, straits, and other geographical features.

Throughout history ship names have been more varied than the names of persons. They petition for safety at sea. They refer to handling qualities, carrying ability, earning power, and beauty. They inform, inspire, honor, threaten. They express love, friendship, trust, confidence, determination. They are as varied as life itself.

Notes

Notes

Books and Journals Abbreviated in the Notes

Ancient Records   James H. Breasted, *Ancient Records of Egypt*, 5 vols. (Chicago, 1906).

Boston-Charlestown Works Progress Administration, *Ship Registers and Enrollments of Boston and Charlestown* (Boston, 1942).

Brooks   F. W. Brooks, *English Naval Forces 1199–1272* (London, 1933).

BWN   T. D. Manning and C. F. Walker, *British Warship Names* (London, 1959).

DANFS   U.S., Navy Department, *Dictionary of American Naval Fighting Ships*, 4 vols. (Washington, D.C., 1959–69).

Hakluyt   Richard Hakluyt, *Voyages*, 8 vols., Everyman's Library (1962).

Jane's   Raymond V. B. Blackman, ed., *Jane's Fighting Ships 1968–69* (New York, 1968).

Lists 5 (I)   R. C. Anderson, *Lists of Men-of-War, 1650–1700: Part I, English Ships, 1649–1702*, Society for Nautical Research, Occasional Publications, no. 5 (London, 1966).

Lists 5 (III)   HJ. Börjeson, P. Holck, W. Vogel, and H. Szymanski, *Lists of Men-of-War, 1650–1700: Part III, Swedish Ships, Danish-Norwegian Ships, German Ships*, Society for Nautical Research, Occasional Publications, no. 5 (London, 1936).

List 7	R. C. Anderson, *List of English Men-of-War 1509–1649*, Society for Nautical Research, Occasional Publications, no. 7 (London, 1959).
Lloyd's	*Lloyd's Register of Shipping 1970–71*, 2 vols. (London, 1970).
Marsden	R. G. Marsden, "English Ships in the Reign of James I," *Transactions of the Royal Historical Society*, n.s. 19 (1905) : 309–42.
MHNY	Works Progress Administration, *A Maritime History of New York* (Garden City, N.Y., 1941).
MM	*The Mariner's Mirror*
Morison	Samuel Eliot Morison, *The Maritime History of Massachusetts* (Boston, 1961).
MVUS68	*Merchant Vessels of the United States, 1968* (Washington, D.C., 1969).
New Orleans	Works Progress Administration, *Ship Registers and Enrollments of New Orleans, La., 1804–1820* (Baton Rouge, 1941).
New York	F. R. Holdcamper, comp., *List of American Flag Merchant Vessels That Received Certificates of Enrollment or Registry at the Port of New York, 1789–1876*, 2 vols. (Washington, D.C., 1968).
Spiegelberg	Wilhelm Spiegelberg, *Rechnungen aus der Zeit Setis I: Mit anderen Rechnungen des neuen Reiches* (Strassburg, 1896).
S–S	Torgny Säve-Söderbergh, "The Navy of the Eighteenth Egyptian Dynasty," *Årsskrift* 6(1946) : 75–90.

Chapter I Naming Theories

4. EMOTIONAL CONTENT

1. Basil Greenhill and Ann Gifford, *The Merchant Sailing Ship* (New York, 1940), p. 78.

5. NAMING ORIGINS

1. James Hornell, *Water Transport: Origins and Early Evolution* (Cambridge, 1946), esp. pp. 272–83.

2. R. C. Anderson, *List of English Men-of-War 1509–1649*, Society for Nautical Research, Occasional Publications, no. 7 (London, 1959) (hereinafter cited as *List 7*).

3. R. C. Anderson, *Lists of Men-of-War, 1650–1700: Part I, English Ships, 1649–1702*, Society for Nautical Research, Occasional Publications, no. 5 (London, 1966) (hereinafter cited as *Lists 5 (I)*).

6. NAME MAGIC AND SECRECY

1. G. L. Canfield and G. W. Dalzell, *The Law of the Sea* (New York, 1921), p. 5.

Chapter II Naming Practices

7. NAMING CEREMONIES

1. Edith E. Benham et al., *Ships of the United States Navy and Their Sponsors, Vol. 1, 1797–1913* (Norwood, Mass., 1913).

2. R. Munro-Smith, *Merchant Ships and Shipping* (London, 1968), p. 155.

8. GOOD NAMES

1. Joseph Conrad, "Initiation: A Discourse Concerning the 'Name' of Ships and the Character of the Sea," *Blackwood's Magazine*, January 1906, p. 6.

2. R. G. Marsden, "English Ships in the Reign of James I," *Transactions of the Royal Historical Society*, n.s. 19 (1905): 309–42 (hereinafter cited as Marsden).

3. E. Arnot Robertson, *The Spanish Town Papers* (London, 1959), p. 134.

4. Rupert S. Holland, *Historic Ships* (Philadelphia, 1926), pp. 82–85.

Chapter III Ancient Ships

9. EGYPT

1. William C. Hayes, *Scepter of Egypt*, 2 vols. (New York, 1953), 1:267.

2. James H. Breasted, *A History of Egypt* (New York, 1967), p. 145.

3. Ibid., p. 225.

4. Palermo stone. See James B. Pritchard, ed., *Ancient Near Eastern Texts Relating to the Old Testament* (Princeton, 1955), p. 227.

5. Torgny Säve-Söderbergh, "The Navy of the Eighteenth Egyptian Dynasty," *Ärsskrift* 6 (1946): 75, 81 (hereinafter cited as S-S).

6. Wilhelm Spiegelberg, *Rechnungen aus der Zeit Setis I: Mit anderen Rechnungen des neuen Reiches* (Strassburg, 1896) (hereinafter cited as Spiegelberg).

7. James H. Breasted, *Ancient Records of Egypt*, 5 vols. (Chicago, 1906) (hereinafter cited as *Ancient Records*).

8. S-S.

9. W. M. F. Petrie, "Boat Names in Egypt," *Ancient Egypt* (London, 1915), pp. 136–37.

10. *Ancient Records*, 1:125.

11. Pritchard, *Ancient Near Eastern Texts*, p. 330; Spiegelberg, p. 81; S–S, p. 83.

12. Spiegelberg, p. 81; S–S, p. 78.

13. *Ancient Records*, 2:6; Spiegelberg, p. 81; S–S, p. 81.

14. *Ancient Records*, 2:6; Spiegelberg, p. 81; S–S, p. 78.

15. *Lloyd's Register of Shipping 1970–71*, 2 vols. (London, 1970) (hereinafter cited as *Lloyd's*).

16. *Ancient Records*, 2:14, 155, 332, 359.

17. *Ancient Records*, 2:139; Spiegelberg, p. 81.

18. S–S, pp. 81, 90; Spiegelberg, pp. 81, 82, 85.

19. S–S, pp. 75, 81, 90.

20. Spiegelberg, p. 82; Pritchard, *Ancient Near Eastern Texts*, p. 330; S–S, pp. 81, 82.

21. *Ancient Records*, 2:349; S-S, pp. 80, 81; Spiegelberg, p. 83.

22. Spiegelberg, pp. 83, 84.

23. Ibid., p. 84.

24. Spiegelberg, pp. 85, 86; S-S, pp. 81, 82.

25. Petrie, "Boat Names in Egypt," pp. 136–37.

26. A. S. Hunt and C. C. Edgar, eds. and trans., *Select Papyri*, 3 vols., Loeb Classical Library (Cambridge, Mass., 1932), 2:459.

10. MESOPOTAMIA

1. Armas Salonen, "Die Wasserfahrzeuge in Babylonien," *Orientalia* 8 (1939):1–160; "Nautica Babylonica," *Orientalia* 11 (1942): esp. 57–65; A. L. Oppenheim, "The Seafaring Merchants of Ur," *American Oriental Society Journal* 74 (1954): 6–17.

2. Theophilus G. Pinches, *Babylonian Tablets of the Berens Collection* (London, 1915), p. 35.

3. Eric Burrows, "Problems of the Absu," *Orientalia* 1 (1932): 236–37.

4. Herbert Kühn, *The Rock Pictures of Europe*, trans. A. H. Brodrick (New York, 1967), p. 187.

5. Wilfred Thesiger, *Marsh Arabs* (New York, 1964).

11. OTHER EAST MEDITERRANEAN PEOPLES

1. A. L. Oppenheim, *The Assyrian Dictionary of the Oriental Institute*, 9 vols. (Chicago, 1958), 4:93.

2. T. H. Gaster, "A Phoenician Naval Gazette: New Light on Homer's Catalogue of Ships," *Quarterly Supplement of the Palestine Exploration Fund*, April 1938, pp. 105–12.

12. GREECE

1. Lionel Casson, *The Ancient Mariners* (New York, 1959), p. 58.

2. Cecil Torr, *Ancient Ships*, ed. A. J. Podlecki (Chicago, 1964), pp. 65–67.

3. J. S. Morrison and R. T. Williams, *Oared Fighting Ships: 900–322 B.C.* (Cambridge, 1968), p. 123.

4. D. M. Robinson, "A New Fragment of the Fifth-Century Athenian Naval Catalogues," *American Journal of Archaeology* 41 (1937):292.

5. [*Corpus*] *inscriptionum Graecarum* (editio minor), II–III, pt. 2, no.1, pp. 184–269.

6. Georges Gustave-Toudouze, *Histoire de la Marine* (Paris, 1934), p. 48.

7. T. D. Manning and C. F. Walker, *British Warship Names* (London, 1959) (hereinafter cited as BWN).

8. *Merchant Vessels of the United States, 1968* (Washington, D.C., 1969) (hereinafter cited as *MVUS68*).

9. Lionel Casson, "The Super-Galleys of the Hellenistic Age," *Mariner's Mirror* 55 (1969): 185–93 (hereinafter cited as *MM*).

10. R. C. Anderson, *Oared Fighting Ships* (London, 1962), p. 21.

13. ROME

1. Silius Italicus, *Punica*, Loeb Classical Library (Cambridge, Mass., 1961).

2. John Nichol, *Historical and Geographical Sources Used by Silius Italicus* (Oxford, 1936).

3. Lucian, *Navigium*, 8 vols., Loeb Classical Library (Cambridge, Mass., 1961), 6:431–39.

4. Lionel Casson, *Illustrated History of Ships and Boats* (New York, 1964), p. 51.

5. *MM* 26 (1940):230.

6. Hunt and Edgar, *Select Papyri*, 1:305.

7. M. Rostovtzeff, *Rome*, trans. J. D. Duff (New York, 1968), p. 236.

8. Ibid., p. 61.

Chapter IV Medieval Ships

14. MEDIEVAL EUROPE

1. Walter Ashburner, *The Rhodian Sea Law* (London, 1909), p. clv.

2. F. W. Brooks, *English Naval Forces 1199–1272* (London, 1933), p. 140 (hereinafter cited as Brooks).

3. Ibid., p. 158.

4. Ibid., p. 184.

5. Philip Cowburn, *The Warship in History* (New York, 1967), p. 50.

6. Brooks, p. 15.

7. Alethea Wiel, *The Navy of Venice* (London, 1910), p. 340.

8. Brooks, p. 24.

9. Lionel Casson, *Illustrated History of Ships and Boats* (New York, 1964), p. 77.

10. Geoffroi de Villehardouin and Sire de Joinville, *Memoirs of the Crusades*, Everyman's Library (New York, 1955), p. 61.

11. Brooks, pp. 27–29.

12. Ibid., pp. 9, 71, 77.

13. Oliver Warner, *Great Sea Battles* (London, 1963), pp. 21–23.

14. W. L. Rodgers, *Naval Warfare under Oars* (Annapolis, 1939), pp. 198–99.

15. Frederic C. Lane, *Venetian Ships and Shipbuilders of the Renaissance* (Baltimore, 1934), pp. 259, 263.

16. Jose Maria Martinez-Hidalgo, *Columbus' Ships* (Barre, Mass., 1966), pp. 46–47.

15. VIKING WARSHIPS

1. A. W. Brögger and H. Shetelig, *The Viking Ships* (Oslo, 1953).

Chapter V Markings—Ancient and Modern

16. Written Names and Other Markings

1. A book by Lionel Casson, *Ships and Seamanship in the Ancient World* (Princeton, 1971), which appeared after completion of this work, devotes a chapter to markings and names of ancient ships. It has an index of about 250 Egyptian, Greek, and Roman names. The selection of Egyptian names is shorter and partly different, and that of the Greek names, longer and partly different, from the names mentioned herein.

2. Alexander McKee, *History under the Sea* (London, 1968), pp. 98–101.

3. H. Szymanski, "The History of Decorated and Coloured Sails," *MM* 13 (1927):164.

4. *MM* 4(1914):157.

5. Hans A. Craemer, *5,000 Jahre Segelschiffe* (Munich-Berlin, 1938).

6. A. Brandt, *Pictorial Treasury of the Marine Museums of the World* (New York, 1967).

7. *List 7.*

8. Great Britain, *Statutes at Large*, 26 George III, c. 60 (1786).

9. Edward Feaser, "H.M.S. *Victory*," *MM* 8(1922):263.

10. U.S., Navy Department, *Dictionary of American Naval Fighting Ships*, 4 vols. (Washington, D.C., 1959–69), 2:581 (hereinafter cited as *DANFS*).

11. Erik Heyl, *Early American Steamers* (Buffalo, 1965), p. 151.

12. Alexander Laing, *American Sail: A Pictorial History* (New York, 1961), p. 192; *American Neptune* 29 (1969): 48, plate VII.

13. Basil Lubbock, *The Romance of the Clipper Ships* (New York, 1958), p. 14.

14. Great Britain, *Public General Statutes*, 36 and 37 Victoria c. 85 (1873).

15. Great Britain, *Public General Acts*, 17 and 18 Victoria c. 104 (1854).

16. Great Britain, *Public General Statutes*, 56 and 58 Victoria c. 60 (1894); 5 and 6 Edward c. 48 (1906).

17. For acts of Congress, by dates cited in text, see *United States Statutes at Large* (Washington, D.C., 1789 to date).

18. *United States Code* (Washington, D.C., 1970).

Chapter VI Modern Ships—Name Sources

17. Name Popularity

1. Works Progress Administration, *Ship Registers and Enrollments of Boston and Charlestown* (Boston, 1942) (hereinafter cited as *Boston-Charlestown*).

2. Works Progress Administration, *Ship Registers of New Bedford, Mass.*, 3 vols. (Boston, 1938).

3. Grahame E. Farr, *Records of Bristol Ships, 1800–1838, Over 150 Tons* (London, 1950).

4. William A. Fairburn, *Merchant Sail*, 6 vols. (Center Lovell, Maine, 1945–55), 4: 2647, 2648, 2651.

19. Christian Names

1. Samuel Eliot Morison, *Admiral of the Ocean Sea* (Boston, 1946), p. 171.

2. *List 7.*

3. Marsden.

4. Henry Hughes, *Immortal Sails* (Lancashire, 1969), p. 204.

5. *Lists 5 (I)*.

6. Marsden.

7. Samuel Eliot Morison, *The Maritime History of Massachusetts* (Boston, 1961), p. 20 (hereinafter cited as Morison).

8. William L. Schurz, *The Manila Galleon* (New York, 1959).

9. Theodore H. Hittell, *Triunfo de la Cruz*, California Historical Society, Special Publications, no. 38 (Los Angeles, 1963).

10. *Lists 5 (I)*.

11. HJ. Börjeson, P. Holck, W. Vogel, and H. Szymanski, *Lists of Men-of-War, 1650–1700: Part III, Swedish Ships, Danish-Norwegian Ships, German Ships,* Society for Nautical Research, Occasional Publications, no. 5 (London, 1936), hereinafter cited as *Lists 5 (III)*.

12. Aletha Weil, *The Navy of Venice* (London, 1910), pp. 298–300.

13. Fishing vessels sailing out of San Pedro, California, 1969.

14. Schurz, *The Manila Galleon*, p. 258.

20. POLITICAL NAMES

1. *BWN*, p. 32.

2. Ralph D. Paine, *The Ships and Sailors of Old Salem* (Chicago, 1912), pp. 500–507.

3. Ibid.

4. *DANFS*, 2:539.

5. Joseph Goldenberg, "Names and Numbers: Statistical Notes on Some Port Records of Colonial North Carolina," *American Neptune* 29 (1969):155–60.

6. Esther Forbes, *Paul Revere and the World He Lived In,* Sentry edition (Boston, 1969), p. 136.

7. Paine, *Ships and Sailors*, pp. 500–507.

8. Ibid.

9. David Syrett, "The Condemnation of the Privateer *Rising States* 1777," *MM* 56 (1970):155.

10. Works Progress Administration, *Newport, R.I., Ship Register 1790–1939* (Providence, 1938–41).

11. Howard I. Chapelle, *The History of the American Sailing Navy* (New York, 1967).

12. Helen Augur, "Benjamin Franklin and the French Alliance," *American Heritage* 7, no. 3 (1956): 67.

13. Howard I. Chapelle, *The Search for Speed under Sail* (New York, 1967), pp. 117–18.

14. *Boston-Charlestown*.

15. *MM* 55(1969): 101.

16. Thomas P. Horgan, *Old Ironsides* (Boston, 1963).

17. William H. Rowe, *The Maritime History of Maine* (New York, 1948), p. 85.

18. Works Progress Administration, *A Maritime History of New York* (Garden City, N.Y., 1941), p. 130 (hereinafter cited as *MHNY*).

19. George Howe, *Mount Hope* (New York, 1959), p. 169.

20. *American Neptune* 29 (1969): 261.

21. Edith E. Benham et al., *Ships of the United States Navy and Their Sponsors*, vol. 1, *1797–1913* (Norwood, Mass., 1913), p. 167.

22. *DANFS*, 2: 563.

23. *Los Angeles Times*, AP, January 31, 1971.

21. Peace, Friendship, Diligence, Profit

1. F. R. Holdcamper, comp., *List of American Flag Merchant Vessels That Received Certificates of Enrollment or Registry at the Port of New York, 1789–1867*, 2 vols. (Washington, D.C., 1968) (hereinafter cited as *New York*).

2. *Boston-Charlestown*.

3. Ibid. Love, Unity, and Treasure could have been person names.

4. Robert Albion, *Square-Riggers on Schedule* (Princeton, 1938), p. 20.

5. Marsden.

6. Ibid.

7. *Boston-Charlestown*.

8. Works Progress Administration, *Ship Registers and Enrollments of New Orleans, La., 1804–1820* (Baton Rouge, 1941) (hereinafter cited as *New Orleans*).

9. Works Progress Administration, *Ship Registers of the District of Plymouth, Mass., 1789–1908* (Boston, 1939).

10. George F. Dow, *The Sailing Ships of New England*, Marine Research Society, Series 3 (Salem, Mass., 1928), p. 24.

11. Works Progress Administration, *Ship Registers and Enrollments of Bristol-Warren, R.I., 1773–1939* (Providence, 1941).

22. Feminine Names

1. Forbes, *Paul Revere*, p. 146.

2. *Inscriptiones Graecae*, XII, pt.1, sec. 712. nos. 56, 65, 75, 78.

3. *New York*.

4. *MM* 8(1922):377.

5. *American Neptune* 29 (1969):159.

6. E. Arnot Robertson, *The Spanish Town Papers* (London, 1959), p. 36.

7. *List 7*.

8. Eileen Power, *Medieval People*, Penguin edition (Harmondsworth, Eng., 1937), p. 136.

9. *New Orleans*.

23. Masculine Names

1. *Merchant Vessels of the United States, 1896* (Washington, D.C., 1897).

2. John P. Cranwell and William B. Crane, *Men of Marque* (New York, 1940), p. 381.

3. *List 7*.

4. *New York*.

24. Place Names

1. *DANFS*, 2:23.

2. Jim Gibbs, *Pacific Square-Riggers* (Seattle, 1969), p. 106.

3. Works Progress Administration, *Ship Registers of New Bedford, Mass.*

25. Abstract Names

1. *MVUS68*.

2. (*Corpus*) *inscriptionum Graecarum* (editio minor) II–III, pt. 2, no.1, pp. 184–269.

3. Breasted, 1:125.

4. Spiegelberg, p. 81.

5. *List 7*.

26. Naval Names

1. Rupert S. Holland, *Historic Ships* (Philadelphia, 1926), p. 318.

2. J. J. Colledge, *Ships of the Royal Navy: An Historical Index*, 2 vols. (New York, 1969–70).

3. T. D. Manning, "Ship Names," *MM* 43 (1957): 91–99.

4. R. W. Neeser, *Ship Names of the United States Navy* (New York, 1921).

5. Edith E. Benham et al., *Ships of the United States Navy and Their Sponsors*, 4 vols. (Norwood, Mass., and Annapolis, 1913–59).

6. William F. Calkins, "Down to the Sea in Ships'—Names," *United States Naval Institute Proceedings*, 84, pt.2 (1958):29–34.

7. "By Any Other Name," *Nation*, July 6, 1918, p. 33.

8. "Bird, Fish or Famous Name Reveal Type of Merchant Ship," *Bureau of Ships Journal* 2, no.5 (1953):24–25.

9. W. H. Mitchell and L. A. Sawyer, *The Liberty Ships: A History of the 'Emergency' Type Cargo Ships Constructed during World War II* (Cambridge, Md., 1970), p. 187.

27. Naval Trophy Names

1. Principal sources for this section: *BWN, DANFS, Jane's* for 1971–72, and *Ships of the Royal Navy* by J. J. Colledge (New York, 1969).

28. Duplicated Warship Names

1. Principal sources for this section: *BWN, DANFS, Jane's* for 1971–72, and *Ships of the Royal Navy* by J. J. Colledge (New York, 1969).

2. Joseph Allen, *Battles of the British Navy*, 2 vols. (London, 1880), 2:121–22.

3. *MM* 22(1936): 240, 359, 360; 23 (1937): 110.

29. Titles—Noble and Otherwise

1. Anders Franzen, *The Warship Vasa* (Stockholm, 1960), p. 7.

2. Alexander Laing, *Clipper Ships and Their Makers* (New York, 1966), p. 299.

30. Heroes and Heroines

1. *DANFS*, 2:265.

2. Ernie Hall, *Flotsam, Jetsam, and Lagan* (Cambridge, Md., 1965), p. 184.

3. Laing, *Clipper Ships*, pp. 100–121.

4. Raymond V. B. Blackman, ed., *Jane's Fighting Ships 1968–69* (New York, 1968) (hereinafter cited as *Jane's*); *Lloyd's*.

5. W. M. Phipps Hornby, "Grace Horsley Darling, 1815–1842, Northumbrian Heroine," *MM* 54 (1968): 55.

6. Works Progress Administration, *Ship Registers and Enrollments of Bristol-Warren, R.I.*

7. Reproduction postcard, Peabody Museum, Salem, Mass.

8. *Merchant Vessels of the United States, 1918* (Washington, D.C., 1919).

9. Works Progress Administration, *Ship Registers and Enrollments of Providence, Rhode Island, 1773–1939* (Providence, 1941).

10. *Lloyd's*, 1948 edition.

11. Morison, p. 351.

12. W. H. Bunting, *Portrait of a Port: Boston, 1852–1914* (Cambridge, Mass., 1971), p. 336.

13. J. S. Tucker, *Memoirs of St Vincent*, 2 vols. (London, 1844), 1:119.

31. DOUBLE NAMES

1. Tom Glasgow, Jr., "The Navy in Philip and Mary's War, 1557–1558," *MM* 53 (1967):328.

2. R. C. Anderson, "Denmark and the First Anglo-Dutch War," *MM* 53 (1967):61.

3. Basil Greenhill and Ann Gifford, *The Merchant Sailing Ship* (New York, 1940), p. 21.

4. Joseph E. Garland, *The Great Patillo* (Boston, 1966), p. 32.

32. FAMILY NAMES

1. Power, *Medieval People*, p. 137.

2. *Lloyd's.*

33. CONSANGUINITY NAMES

1. *New York*; Works Progress Administration, *Alphabetical List of Ship Registers, District of Barnstable, Mass., 1814–1913* (Boston, 1938).

2. Dana T. Bowen, *Lore of the Lakes* (Daytona Beach, 1940), p. 87.

34. TYPE NAMES

1. Robertson, *Spanish Town Papers*, p. 64.

2. Morison, p. 305.

3. Frank O. Braynard, *Famous American Ships* (New York, 1956), p. 27.

4. Lionel Casson, *Illustrated History of Ships and Boats* (New York, 1964), p. 211.

5. John Guthrie, *Bizarre Ships of the Nineteenth Century* (New York, 1970), p. 75.

6. *Lists 5 (I)*; *List 7.*

7. *Lists 5 (III).*

35. FUNCTION or CARGO

1. Leslie Baird, "POP—Perpendicular Ocean Platform," *Sea Frontiers* 14 (1968): 210.

2. *Los Angeles Times*, June 7, 1970.

3. *MHNY*, p. 102.

4. *Lists 5 (I).*

5. C. W. Rush, W. C. Chamblis, and H. J. Gimpel, *Complete Book of Submarines* (Cleveland, 1958), p. 13.

6. *MHNY*, pp. 312–14.

7. *Lloyd's.*

8. Carl Cutler, *Greyhounds of the Sea* (New York, 1930), pp. 419, 431, 438.

9. *MHNY*, p. 131.

10. *New York.*

11. *Boston-Charlestown.*

12. Morison, p. 59.

13. Frederick C. Matthews, *American Merchant Ships 1850–1900* (Salem, 1930), pp. 162–64.

14. Fairburn, *Merchant Sail*, 4: 2652.

15. Works Progress Administration, *Ship Registers: Port of Philadelphia* (Philadelphia, 1942).

16. Edward Lewis and Robert O'Brien, *Ships* (New York, 1968), p. 118.

36. PAIRED NAMES

1. Richard Hakluyt, *Voyages*, 8 vols., Everyman's Library (1962) (hereinafter cited as Hakluyt).

2. M. V. Brewington, *Chesapeake Bay: A Pictorial Maritime History* (Cambridge, Md., 1953), p. 7.

3. Corey Ford, *Where the Sea Breaks Its Back* (Boston, 1966), p. 36.

4. Woodes Rogers, *A Cruising Voyage round the World* (New York, 1922), p. 2.

5. Donald C. Cutter, *Malaspina in California* (San Francisco, 1960).

6. Basil Lubbock, *The China Clippers* (Boston, 1925), p. 132.

7. Braynard, *Famous American Ships*, p. 140.

8. Ibid., p. 151.

9. Alan Mitchell, *Splendid Sisters* (London, 1966).

10. *Lloyd's*.

37. SERIES NAMES

1. George Goldsmith-Carter, *Sailors Sailors* (London, 1966), p. 56.

2. George Howe, *Mount Hope* (New York, 1959), p. 135.

3. Rowe, *Maritime History of Maine*, p. 58.

4. Fairburn, *Merchant Sail,* 4:2616.

5. Ibid., 4:2652.

6. H. C. Paul Rohrback, *FL: A Century and a Quarter of Reederei F. Laeisz* (Flagstaff, Ariz., 1957), p. 18.

7. A. G. Course, *Windjammers of the Horn* (London, 1969), pp. 73, 94.

8. Neil Potter and Jack Frost, *The Mary* (London, 1961), pp. 85–89.

9. Eugene W. Smith, *Passenger Ships of the World: Past and Present* (Boston, 1963), pp. 688, 691, 717.

10. Ibid., pp. 698, 175.

11. Laurence Dunn, *The World's Tankers* (Garden City, N.Y., 1967), p. 18.

38. SAFE RETURN

1. *New Orleans*.

2. Marsden.

3. Hakluyt.

4. *Lists 5 (I)*.

5. *Lloyd's*.

6. *MVUS68*.

39. EXPLORATION AND SCIENCE

1. Hakluyt.

2. Alan Villiers, *Captain James Cook* (New York, 1967).

3. Ernest S. Dodge, *Beyond the Capes* (Boston, 1971), p. 273.

4. G. S. Nares, *A Voyage to the Polar Sea*, 2 vols. (London, 1878), 1:112–14.

5. *Encyclopaedia Britannica* (1970) s.v. "Antarctica."

6. *Science News* 99(1971): 388.

7. Cutter, *Malaspina in California.*

8. E. G. Ravenstein, ed. and trans., *A Journal of the First Voyage of Vasco da Gama* (London, 1898), p. 1.

9. Hakluyt.

10. *Bol'shaia sovetskaia ensiklopediia* (1950) s.v. "Tchirikoff."

11. Rush, Chamblis, and Gimpel, *Submarines,* p. 16.

40. Unusual Names

1. *List 7.*

2. Ibid.

3. Ibid.

4. *MM* 43 (1957): 91–99.

5. *List 7.*

6. Marsden.

7. *List 7.*

8. *Lists 5 (III)*; Pierre Le Conte, *Lists of Men-of-War, 1650–1700: Part II, French Ships, 1648–1700,* Society for Nautical Research, Occasional Publications, no. 5 (London, 1935); A. Vreugdenhil, *Lists of Men-of-War, 1650–1700: Part IV, Ships of the United Netherlands, 1648–1702* (London, 1938).

9. *Jane's.*

10. *MHNY,* p. 39.

11. *Lists 5 (I).*

12. *MHNY,* p. 125.

13. Robertson, *Spanish Town Papers,* pp. 113, 157.

14. Morison, p. 200.

15. Howe, *Mount Hope,* p. 120.

16. *New Orleans.*

17. Alexander Laing, *American Sail: A Pictorial History* (New York, 1961), p. 159.

18. Cranwell and Crane, *Men of Marque,* p. 313.

19. Chapelle, *American Sailing Navy,* p. 339.

20. Brewington, *Chesapeake Bay,* p. 78.

21. Braynard, *Famous American Ships,* p. 37.

22. Marsden.

23. Ibid.

24. *New Orleans.*

25. Rowe, *Maritime History of Maine,* pp. 125, 250.

26. *Lists 5 (I).*

27. *New York.*

28. *New Orleans.*

29. Chapelle, *Search for Speed under Sail,* p. 280.

30. Ibid., p. 395.

31. Morison, p. 339.

32. Gibbs, *Pacific Square-Riggers,* p. 163.

33. Frederick W. Wallace, *Wooden Ships and Iron Men* (Boston, 1937), pp. 328–29.

34. *DANFS,* 2:93.

35. *Yachting* 20, no.5 (1916): 197.
36. Marsden.

41. CONTEMPORARY INFLUENCES

1. Gibbs, *Pacific Square-Riggers*, p. 172.
2. Laing, *Clipper Ships*, p. 172.
3. Morison, p. 348.
4. Works Progress Administration, *Ship Registers, District of Barnstable, Mass.*
5. *American Neptune* 27(1967): 99.
6. Ibid., 28 (1968): 122.
7. Marsden.

Chapter VII Name Forms

42. THE DEFINITE ARTICLE

1. Leland P. Lovette, *Naval Customs, Traditions, and Usage* (Annapolis, 1934), p. 277.
2. Basil Lubbock, *The Romance of the Clipper Ships* (New York, 1958), p. 20.

44. ADJECTIVE NAMES

1. *List 7.*
2. Marsden.
3. *MM* 54 (1968): 129.
4. Ibid., 8 (1922): 29.
5. *BWN.*
6. *List 7.*
7. *BWN.*
8. *MM* 57(1971):57.
9. *DANFS*, 1:157.
10. *List 7.*

45. VERB NAMES

1. William L. Schurz, *The Manila Galleon* (New York, 1959), pp. 307–13.
2. *Lists 5 (I).*
3. Howard I. Chapelle, *The Search for Speed under Sail* (New York, 1967), p. 195.
4. Ibid., p. 229.
5. George G. Putnam, *Salem Vessels and Their Voyages* (Salem, Mass., 1924), p. 64.
6. Morison, p. 306.
7. *MM* 57(1971):8.
8. *DANFS*, 1:13.

47. NUMERICAL NAMES

1. *MM* 56(1970):27.
2. *MM* 43(1957):99.

3. *Lists 5 (III).*

4. Howard I. Chapelle, *The History of the American Sailing Navy* (New York, 1967), p. 282.

5. Alexander Laing, *American Sail: A Pictorial History* (New York, 1961), pp. 138–45.

6. *DANFS*, 2:316.

7. *DANFS*, 2:575.

48. NICKNAMES

1. Frank C. Bowen, *America Sails the Seas* (New York, 1938), p. 278.

2. *DANFS*, 2:170.

3. Alethea Wiel, *The Navy of Venice* (London, 1910), p. 121.

4. Ernie Hall, *Flotsam, Jetsam, and Lagan* (Cambridge, Md., 1965), pp. 188–90.

5. Leonard V. Huber, "Heyday of the Floating Palace," *American Heritage* 8, no.6 (1957): 98.

6. Jean de la Varende, *Cherish the Sea: A History of Sail* (New York, 1956), p. 237.

7. Stanley Rogers, *Freak Ships* (London, 1936), p. 14.

8. Dwight Boyer, *Great Stories of the Great Lakes* (New York, 1966), p. 6.

9. Allan R. Bosworth, *My Love Affair with the Navy* (New York, 1969), p. 184.

10. Samuel Eliot Morison, *Admiral of the Ocean Sea* (Boston, 1946), p. 395.

11. William F. Calkins, "Down to the Sea in Ships'—Names," *United States Naval Institute Proceedings* 84, pt.2 (1958): 34.

12. *MM* 57(1971):232.

13. W. H. Bunting, *Portrait of a Port: Boston, 1852–1914* (Cambridge, Mass., 1971), p. 402.

14. *MM* 45(1959):154, 337–38.

49. SURROGATE NAMES

1. Leonard V. Huber, "Heyday of the Floating Palace," *American Heritage* 8, no.6 (1957): 98.

2. George H. Preble, *Origin and History of the American Flag*, 2 vols. (Philadelphia, 1917), 2:662.

3. M. V. Brewington, "Signal Systems and Ship Identification," *American Neptune* 3(1943):205–20.

50. NAME BADGES

1. Gervis Frere-Cook, *The Decorative Arts of the Mariner* (Boston, 1966).

2. Alfred E. Weightman, *Heraldry in the Royal Navy: Crests and Badges of H. M. Ships* (Aldershot, 1957).

3. H. Gresham Carr, *Flags of the World* (New York, 1961), p. 187.

51. HERALDIC NAMES

1. *List 7.*

2. *Lists 5 (I).*

3. Samuel Eliot Morison, *The European Discovery of America: The Northern Voyages* (New York, 1971), pp. 126, 568.

Chapter VIII Miscellany

52. SUPERSTITIONS

   1. Hakluyt.

   2. Dana T. Bowen, *Lore of the Lakes* (Daytona Beach, 1940), p. 303.

   3. William A. Fairburn, *Merchant Sail*, 6 vols. (Center Lovell, Maine, 1945–55), 4: 2653.

   4. *MM* 43(1957): 97.

   5. Dwight Boyer, *Great Stories of the Great Lakes* (New York, 1966), pp. 71–74.

   6. Jim Gibbs, *Pacific Square-Riggers* (Seattle, 1969), p. 97.

   7. Basil Lubbock, *The Down Easters* (Glasgow, 1923), p. 108.

   8. *MVUS68*.

53. NAME CHANGES

   1. J. C. Furnas, "The Names We Go By," *Saturday Evening Post* 230 (1957): 36, 37, 71.

   2. Noah J. Jacobs, *Naming Day in Eden* (New York, 1969), p. 29.

   3. Athenaeus, *The Deipnosophists*, 7 vols., Loeb Classical Library (New York, 1927), 2:445.

   4. "The Maiden Names of Presidents," *Nation* 114 (1922): 640.

   5. Furnas, "The Names We Go By."

   6. *MHNY*, p. 257.

   7. G. F. Hammond, "Tell 'Em We're the Coast Guard," *Skipper*, December 1969, p. 39.

   8. *American Neptune* 29(1969):195.

   9. *Lists 5 (I)*.

   10. *BWN*, pp. 29–30.

   11. Edgar K. Thompson, "A Strange Case in Admiralty," *MM* 55(1969):455.

   12. Basil Lubbock, *The Last of the Windjammers*, 2 vols. (Boston, 1929), 2:62.

   13. Alan Villiers, *Captain James Cook* (New York, 1967), pp. 183–84.

   14. Henry B. Culver, *Forty Famous Ships* (Garden City, N.Y., 1936), p. 145.

   15. Ibid., p. 163.

   16. Basil Lubbock, *Log of the Cutty Sark* (Glasgow, 1960), pp. 33–34, 233, 291.

   17. *Lloyd's Register of Shipping, 1873* (London, 1873).

   18. *Lloyd's Register of Shipping, 1870* (London, 1870).

   19. Gibbs, *Pacific Square-Riggers*, p. 76.

   20. Ibid., p. 147.

54. SHIP SURGERY NAMES

   1. L. A. Sawyer and W. H. Mitchell, *Merchant Ships of the World: Tankers* (New York, 1967), pp. 95, 105.

   2. *New York Times*, June 15, 1941.

   3. *Wall Street Journal*, January 26, 1971.

55. YACHTS

   1. *Lloyd's Register of American Yachts* (New York, 1939–70).

56. "Maru"

1. *Daijiten*, 26 vols. (Tokyo, 1953–54), 23:542; *New Japanese-English Dictionary* (Tokyo, 1954); *MM* 1 (1911):287; interview with Che-Hwei Lin, Oriental Library, University of California, Los Angeles.

2. R. Munro-Smith, *Merchant Ships and Shipping* (London, 1968), p. 153.

Chapter IX Namers

57. Ships That Gave Their Names

1. Alexander Laing, *American Sail: A Pictorial History* (New York, 1961), p. 91.

2. Samuel Eliot Morison, *By Land and By Sea* (New York, 1953), p. 137.

3. Ibid., p. 140.

4. Ibid., p. 133.

5. *Encyclopaedia Britannica* (1970) s.v. "William E. Parry."

6. Charles Darwin, *A Naturalist's Voyage round the World in H.M.S. "Beagle"* (London, 1930), p. 223.

7. Max Miller, *California's Secret Islands* (New York, 1971), pp. 178–81.

8. *Science News* 99(1971): 385.

9. Jerry MacMullen, "A Landlocked and Very Good Harbor," *Westways*, August 1969, p. 65.

10. Henry B. Culver, *Forty Famous Ships* (New York, 1936), p. 134.

11. John Guthrie, *Bizarre Ships of the Nineteenth Century* (Cranbury, N.J., 1971), pp. 156–61.

12. Frank O. Braynard, *Famous American Ships* (New York, 1956), p. 171.

13. Ernie Hall, *Flotsam, Jetsam, and Lagan* (Cambridge, Md., 1965), p. 242.

14. Charles B. Cross, Jr., *The Chesapeake: A Biography of a Ship* (Chesapeake, Va., 1968), p. 70.

58. Some Famous Namers

1. Culver, *Forty Famous Ships*, p. 49.

2. *MM* 56(1970): 11.

3. Anders Franzen, *The Warship Vasa* (Stockholm, 1960), p. 7.

4. *BWN*.

5. Culver, *Forty Famous Ships*, p. 125.

6. Humphreys to Secretary of War, February 20, 1795, Joshua Humphreys Papers, Historical Society of Pennsylvania, cited in *American Neptune* 7(1947): 255.

7. *MM* 55(1969): 210.

8. Robert Carse, *The Moonrakers* (New York, 1961), p. 38.

9. Braynard, *Famous American Ships*, p. 96.

10. John Robinson and G. F. Dow, *The Sailing Ships of New England*, Marine Research Society, 2d ser. (Salem, Mass., 1924), p. 22.

11. Peter Gretton, *Former Naval Person: Winston Churchill and the Royal Navy* (London, 1968), pp. 86–88.

12. *BWN*, p. 58.

13. *American Neptune* 22(1936):276.

14. Braynard, *Famous American Ships*, p. 176.

15. Edith Bolling Wilson, *My Memoir* (New York, 1939), pp. 140–41.

16. Ibid., p. 166.

59. FICTIONAL SHIPS, MOSTLY REAL NAMES

1. *Merchant Vessels of the United States, 1867–68* (Washington, D.C., 1868).

2. J. J. Colledge, *Ships of the Royal Navy: An Historical Index*, 2 vols. (New York, 1969–70).

3. William A. Fairburn, *Merchant Sail*, 6 vols. (Center Lovell, Maine, 1945–55), 3: 1765.

Indexes

Subject Index

Ship Names Index

Note: One name entry may refer to several different ships, perhaps on same page; (lit.) indicates a name from literature, which may also be an actual ship name.